GIVEN AND SENT IN ONE LOVE

The True Church of Jesus Christ

By Gerrit Scott Dawson
and Mark R. Patterson

Edited, with an introduction, by Craig M. Kibler
Foreword by Anita Bell and Jerry Andrews
Afterword by Parker T. Williamson

REFORMATION PRESS

Reformation Press
P.O. Box 2210
136 Tremont Park Drive
Lenoir, North Carolina 28645

Reformation Press books, monographs and other resources are avail-able at special discounts in bulk purchases for educational and min-istry use. For more details, contact:

Director of Publications
Reformation Press
P.O. Box 2210
136 Tremont Park Drive
Lenoir, North Carolina 28645

Call us at 1-800-368-0110

Or visit Reformation Press on the Web at www.resourcecatalog.org

Cover Design: HeuleGordon, Inc.; Grand Rapids, Michigan

Printed in the United States of America

TABLE OF CONTENTS

FOREWORD

C hurch policy papers usually serve some purpose in the Church, but seldom is that purpose significant Biblical exposition, seen through the lens of inspired and faithful theological reasoning, toward the end of bold and committed action.

Having carefully followed the work of the Theological Task Force on Peace, Unity and Purity of the Presbyterian Church (USA) – its commission, meetings and interim reports – the Board of Directors of the Presbyterian Coalition was concerned that an opportunity for important reflection on the nature and calling of the Church might be missed. We feared that the task force's final report would be marked by too much attention to the surface quakings, with too little attention paid to the shifting tectonic plates beneath; too much sacrificed for consensus, with too little committed to clarity; too careful an avoidance of measuring the chasm within the church, with too casual a commitment to the world beyond.

Our concern was that the task force's final report too easily could be satisfied by agreeing to disagree, while being too hesitant to decide. Indeed, we thought it possible for the task force to fulfill the commission of the General Assembly, yet offer the Church less than what the Church needs in this hour.

The Board of Directors of the Presbyterian Coalition discerned that the time had come to reframe the question before the Church from institutional survival to the nature and calling of the church. To this end, we invited theological reflection that would culminate in an offering – Biblically framed, clearly written and grounded in the faith of the ancients. We trusted that such an offering would stimulate original thinking and inspire faithful action.

Two pastor-theologians, Gerrit Scott Dawson and Mark R. Patterson, accepted this challenging invitation to engage in seminal work that would be offered as a gift to the whole Church. Their papers, "Given and Sent in One Love: The True Church of Jesus Christ" and "Gracious

Act – Gracious Response: The Character of the Church Under God's Redeeming Love," provide a teaching moment for us all. These papers are fresh, yet recognize the faith of the Church; they are original, but not idiosyncratic. They offer vision and calling to revive the Church.

We hope you will give these papers a careful read, considering the call to action found within their pages. We hope they will further the Church's ongoing and necessary work of recapturing an ecclesiology that is at once catholic and apostolic, Reformed and evangelical. We hope the Biblical vision woven within them will further the peace, unity and purity of the Church.

Toward that end, we recommend these essays to you. We are grateful for the sacrifice of Gerrit Scott Dawson and Mark R. Patterson in faithful service of the Savior.

Anita Bell
Oreland, Pennsylvania

Jerry Andrews
Glen Ellyn, Illinois

Co-moderators
The Presbyterian Coalition

Introduction

"Did God really say ...?"

Jesus Christ is being replaced by "Christianity," a religion whose revisionists make partial use of his name. Whether by cultural osmosis or mistaken loyalty to a religious institution whose leaders have forgotten "the faith that was once for all delivered to the saints,"[1] many self-identified Christians pursue a way of life that bears faint resemblance to the Gospel. They do this by amending the Word of God to bolster an alternative religion of their own making.

The temptation toward amendment is not new. When the serpent asked Eve, "Did God really say, 'You shall not eat of any tree in the garden?'"[2] Eve, knowing God allowed the fruit of every tree except one to be eaten, did not deny the Word of God outright but twisted it – quoting a portion, but not the whole. Tempted by half-truth, Eve sidestepped the divine injunction, "But of the tree of the knowledge of good and evil you shall not eat, for in the day that you eat of it you shall surely die."[3]

This ancient deception has resurfaced in modern times with a vengeance. Having failed in their unrelenting frontal assaults on the truth, denominational revisionists of the Gospel now employ the serpent's tactic, increasingly described as "a third way." Outright denials of God's truth – e.g., faddish "God is dead" theologies in the sixties, "Voices of Sophia" demonstrations in the 1990s, and "What's the big deal about Jesus?" themes in the early 2000s – did not gain traction among Presbyterians in the pews, despite their promotion by some Presbyterian leaders. Such blatant attacks on the Church's faith summarily were rejected by its people because these attacks so obviously deny the plain meaning of the Gospel. These failures have led those who share such views to choose a more subtle approach, one that employs the

---

1. Jude 3.
2. Genesis 3:1.
3. Genesis 2:17.

faith's vocabulary while twisting its meaning. Mainline denominations in North America and Europe have been particularly susceptible to the venom that such "third way" tactics have injected into their institutional bloodstreams.

Accommodating to culture, ecclesiastical bureaucracies have become an integral part of what Garry Wills calls the "structures of deceit."[4] This is not as simple as blatant lying, Wills says. People who sincerely believe in these things are subverted to "quiet cosmetic labors buttressing the church by 'improving' its substructure. These continual readjustments of the foundation are bound to weaken it, while destroying any standards for honest workmanship in those who think they are saving their church by fiddling it into intellectual irrelevance."

In Presbyterian circles, people who do such things often describe their position as "reformed and always reforming." This description distorts the Reformed tradition's dictum: "reformed and always being reformed by the Word of God." On first hearing, the revisionists' version sounds similar to the original, but it actually is quite different. Human ingenuity is not the source of reformation. We do not reform ourselves. Instead, we are being reformed by the truth that comes from beyond us. Secondly, the new life that we experience in reformation is no mere novelty. There are clear limits to the nature and extent of one's reformation. For the Christian, reformation occurs according "to the Word of God."

Versions of faith that are proffered to Presbyterians today are not so much apostasy (the blatant denial of truth) as they are heresy (the distortion of it). Heresy, by comparison, is more difficult to discern because it employs the language of the faith. Some of its assertions, in fact, are true, but, when mixed with falsehood, result in the denial of truth.

In 325 A.D., an ordained deacon named Arius promulgated a heresy whose popularity among church leaders inflicted a devastating wound to the early church. Heavily influenced by Greek philosophy, Arius believed that the spiritual and material realms must be absolutely distinct, and that any attempt to conjoin them was impossible. Thus, he could not accept the Gospel's claim that God was incarnate in Jesus Christ.

Had Arius simply claimed that the Gospel is false (apostasy), he would have been drummed out of the church for denying an essential tenet of the Christian faith. So he employed a different tactic. He

---

4.   Wills, Garry; *Papal Sin* (Image Books; New York; 2001); p. 7.

affirmed that he believed Jesus was the Son of God. Then he proceeded to redefine "sonship." The Son, he argued, is not of the same essence as the Father. Thus, Son became an honorific title, bestowed on an exemplary human being in recognition of his God-like life.

In his declaration that Jesus Christ is the Son of God, this popular preacher pleased many Christians in his audience who failed to hear his subtle nuances. His sermons included many things with which Christians could agree. But, as his chief critic Athanasius proved during subsequent debates, these common affirmations were employed by Arius to obscure a pivotal point of divergence between those who saw Jesus Christ as a moral hero and those who believed he was of one substance with the Father.

In reading a report issued in September 2005 by the Theological Task Force on Peace, Unity and Purity of the Presbyterian Church (USA), one is reminded of the Arian heresy. Promoted as a solution to the divisions that are tearing the denomination asunder, the task force's report includes statements of faith that would cause orthodox Christians to rejoice. For undiscerning readers, this partial inclusion of truth obscures fatal distortions of God's Word that occur elsewhere in the report, as well as its being based on an un-Biblical methodology that offers equal status to truth and falsehood.

Given and Sent in One Love: The True Church of Jesus Christ could not have come at a more propitious moment. In this volume, Gerrit Scott Dawson and Mark R. Patterson take seriously the plight of the Presbyterian Church (USA) that gave birth to its task force. But unlike the task force, these two pastor-theologians approach the task of discerning the church's peace, unity and purity by addressing the *whole* counsel of God. Dawson and Patterson resist the temptation to throw Biblical proof texts at convictions drawn from un-Biblical sources. Instead, they turn directly to Scripture and to the Triune God of Grace.

Dawson says that the solution to forgetting the *whole* counsel of God "lies in the great resources of the Church: the gift of the Holy Spirit, the Holy Scriptures and the historic confessions." He reminds us that, "The Church is the Creation of the Triune God, called into being and sent into the world as Father, Son and Holy Spirit to glorify one another in dynamic love."

All of us, he writes, "have our life together always and only as recipients of grace that is not of our devising or deserving. We are the outworking of the divine love as it was and is expressed in the field of our humanity, in the world where we live."

Patterson is just as emphatic about the grace of God:

"The loss of peace, unity and purity [in the Church] are inevitable wherever and whenever the church misunderstands, rejects, annuls, or redefines the grace of God made ours in Christ. Within the Catholic, Protestant and Reformed traditions, grace is the defining characteristic of both God's act on our behalf and the character of our relationship with him.

"Grace is the singularly precise description of God's work of redemption and our response of repentance and faith. Grace is a concrete reality flowing from the nature of God and manifesting itself precisely and efficaciously in the person and work of the Son. Grace, having its source in the being and will of the Father and manifesting itself in the Son, becomes, by the act of the Spirit, a transformative reality by which our relationship with God is restored and our lives redeemed."

Not surprisingly, Dawson and Patterson arrive at a very different place than does the denomination's task force. Theirs is no cultural accommodation for the sake of preserving an ecclesiastical institution. Theirs is an insistence that worldly words are no match for the Word of God. They insist that Scripture – *all* of it – says what it means and means what it says. In so doing, they affirm a timeless vision of the Church for the 21st century:

> "We do not want, as the newspapers say, a Church that will move with the world. We want a Church that will move the world ... It is by that test that history will really judge, of any Church, whether it is the real Church or no."[5]

Craig M. Kibler
Patterson, North Carolina

---

5.   Ffinch, Michael; *G.K. Chesterton: A Biography* (San Francisco; Harper & Row; 1986); p. 277.

Book One

Given and Sent in One Love

The True Church of Jesus Christ

TABLE OF CONTENTS

Chapter One

THE NATURE OF OUR CONFLICT

In the days of our denominational decline, the question is torn from our lips, "Where did we go wrong?" The season of our controversy shows little sign of abating. From every side, bone-weary, we wonder, "Is the church *supposed* to be like this?"

We try to figure out how a denomination called the Presbyterian Church (USA) relates to the Church of Jesus Christ, the one holy, catholic and apostolic Church throughout all time and space. We know that a corporation begun in 1983 is but a human construct. People created the documents that joined us; people can redraw their terms at any time, just like any other American corporation. Yet, if the PC(USA) were nothing more than a business, why does it matter so much to us? We know in our souls that something related to the eternal Church is at stake in our denominational struggle. Something deeper than property rights, or even ordination standards, stirs in the heart of our debates.

As we read Scripture, we understand that spiritual conflict is a continuing reality. Until the return of Christ Jesus, his Church is engaged in a struggle, not "against flesh and blood, but against the rulers, against the authorities, against the cosmic powers over this present darkness, against the spiritual forces of evil in the heavenly realms."[1] This conflict occurs as the Church, bearing witness to Jesus the Light of the world, engages that same world that is shrouded in a darkness that does not willingly recede. Moreover, our enemy's "craft and power are great."[2] From early on, this spiritual struggle has been engaged within – and not

---

1. Ephesians 6:12.

2. *A Mighty Fortress Is Our God.* Words and music by Martin Luther (1529); Stanza 1, line 4.

just without – the boundaries of the Church.

The storm within the PC(USA) partakes of this cosmic conflict. Among kind people of good will, starkly different assertions of truth are pitted against one another. These worldviews at odds within our denomination are incompatible. Without a resolution to the conflict, the energy of our churches will continue to be diverted from our Gospel mission to the world as we fight among each other. Even if we simply try to get along by declining to engage over our differences, the denomination will fail. In an enforced but false peace, disparate visions will continue to shape the church. To a lost world, we will present churches that either stand for everything (and, thus, for nothing) or appear schizophrenic in their vision for what it means to follow Christ. The time has come to unmask the spiritual issues at stake and to understand the choices before us.

The conflict itself, however, is not our core problem. The continuing battle is a symptom of the fact that we as a denomination have allowed error – in belief and practice – to persist within our common life. We are ill as a denomination because we have brought distortions of the truth within the bosom of the Church. Why have we not brought loving, godly discipline to bear upon these alien influences? Perhaps we simply have not had the collective will to do so. Or perhaps, having the will, we have lacked the power or the skill. A debilitating fever continues when the body is fighting off a virulent disease. In the same way, our denomination is weak and feverish from trying to conduct its life and mission at the same time that beliefs and practices alien to historic Christianity circulate throughout our churches. How will we be healed?

Thankfully, the Church is not without healing resources. Truth can be discerned from error; right practice can be distinguished from wrong. The Holy Scriptures of the Old and New Testaments have been given to the people of God. The blessed Holy Spirit has been poured upon the Church to lead us into all truth. The faithful throughout the generations have made bold confessions of faith. In doing so, they have marked out the boundaries of faithful interpretation of the Scriptures. We *can* know the truth that leads us to personally know the Triune God and the pattern of faithful Christian living. Through that truth, our God will make us well again.

In order for that to happen, however, we must employ the resources given to the Church. We are summoned to the humility of acknowledging the truth that is not of our making and to consecrating our lives to the truth that God has made known. We then are called to declare that truth boldly and in love to the Church and to the world. In that act, the way of our future as a denomination will be made clear. We will know whether the illness of this denomination is unto death and, hence, dissolution; or whether we will be led to healing and, thus, life together.

To undertake this task of discerning truth in order that we might declare truth, we will think *theologically* about the Church. We will draw from the deep well of Holy Scripture, particularly Jesus' prayer for his disciples in John 17 and its larger context of John 13-17. We will consider in turn:

- The Nature of the Church: The Gift of the Triune God.
- The Peace of the Church.
- The Purity of the Church.
- The Unity of the Church.
- The Alien Atmosphere our Denomination Breathes.
- A Plan for Faithful Action Patterned after Acts 15-16.

Chapter Two

THE NATURE OF THE CHURCH: THE GIFT OF THE TRIUNE GOD

The Church is the creation of the Triune God, called into being and sent into the world as Father, Son and Holy Spirit to glorify one another through the Church in dynamic love.

On the night in which the conflict between the powers of darkness and the Light of the world reached its height, our Lord made his prayers for his church. The high priestly prayer of John 17 forms a majestic conclusion. We overhear the intimacy of Jesus' relationship with his Father and how our lives as his people are taken up into that love. The life of the Father and the Son in the bonds of the Spirit is the context in which the Church has her life and, actually, is the only way the nature of the Church properly can be understood.

We confess, of course, to be Trinitarians. We believe that the one God has his being in the three persons of Father, Son and Holy Spirit. In practice, however, we more often act as unitarians, rarely thinking through what the tri-unity of God means for our life together, our worship and our mission. Yet, we have to do the hard work of thinking in Trinitarian terms if we are to penetrate to the meaning of the Church that Jesus gave the world. Out of that depth, the true definitions of our peace, purity and unity will arise. Then, and only then, will we discern the resolution to our conflict.

Listening in on the prayer of John 17, we discover that our life together in Christ is actually taken up into *the eternal story of the relationship between the Father and the Son.* Jesus prayed, "And now, Father, glorify me in your own presence with the glory that I had with you before the world existed."[1] We immediately notice the eternal dimensions of this love story. The intimacy between the Father and the Son flourished before the world was made. It always has been. Father and Son forever have been giving glory to one another.

This eternal love also had a very present dimension in Jesus' prayer since his impending betrayal and arrest would lead to the paradox of Jesus' glory as he determined to be faithful even unto the shame of the cross. And we note an everlasting future dimension to their love as Jesus prepared to return to the immediate presence of his Father. Earlier, John began the account of the foot washing by saying, "Jesus, knowing the Father had given all things into his hands, and that he had come from God, and was going back to God. ..."[2] In his prayer, Jesus was aware that he had an eternal existence as the Son of God before his incarnation, that his relationship with his Father had continued in unbroken faithfulness through his sojourn among us, and that he would soon resume his place in the immediate presence of his Father. The difference, however, between the love of eternity past and that future with his Father is that Jesus continues to remain united to the humanity he assumed from us. He has taken what we are up into the life of dynamic love and shared glory with his Father.

Though this consideration of the Trinity can threaten to shut down our minds with complicated abstractions, we must carry on. Considering the Triune nature of God, through the narrative of his actions in relation to the world, can help us stay focused. We may discern the *story structure* revealed in the all-important Scripture, "God is love."[3] Love involves relationship. God is a being in relationship. Within the one God, there are three persons – Father, Son and Holy Spirit. Each is fully, truly God. Each is a person. The Father loves the Son and has from all eternity. He delights to share his divine life with him. The Son loves the Father, and delights to please him, to give himself in obedience. The Spirit loves the Father and the Son and rejoices to be given as the love between them. Such obedience is not, however, lived in the way we ordinarily think of it as between employer and worker, coach and player, or even parent and child. This obedience and self-giving is between equals – equals who find delight in freely offering themselves to one another.

It is the nature of love to be turned out from oneself toward the other.

---

1.   John 17:5.

2.   John 12:3.

3.   1 John 4:18.

Love is only love when there is someone to love. As the Father, Son and Holy Spirit loved one another in perfect joy and delight and fulfillment, the God who is three, who is one, decided that this love could be magnified if it overflowed in creation. We read in Genesis 1:26, "Then God said, 'Let us make man in our image, after our likeness.'" Within that remarkable plural "our" of God's counsel came the creation of the man and woman who, together, form the image of God. We have been granted a real existence. We live in dependence on the Triune God, but are not merely part of him. Out of his own communion of love, God created us to be able to love him freely in return. He gave us the capacity for speech so that we might converse with him and one another. Moreover, new life springs forth from the love of a man and a woman as the image of this life-creating, overflowing love of the Triune God.

In this love, it came to pass that the world was created. Of course, we chose against freely living in the obedience that comprises loving fellowship with the Triune God. With our sin, estrangement from God and one another ensued. Death entered the world. We were cut off from fulfilling our original purpose.

The God of grace, however, did not cease loving us and did not leave us alone but, instead, sent us prophets and leaders to teach us of his love. So "for us and for our salvation,"[4] in the fullness of time, the Triune God according to his eternal counsel brought the love that flows between the divine persons right down into our midst.

The Father sent the Son through the Spirit to enter the world in human flesh and bones. The Son loves his Father as he has from all eternity but, since the incarnation, he has done so from *inside* our humanity. From his position as the man Jesus, the Son loves his Father and obeys him and rejoices in his love.

Our story, then, is about what happened when the love between Father and Son was fleshed out within our world. As the Son took up our humanity, joining himself to us, our humanity was taken up in the interplay of love between the divine persons.

In these amazing days, the Father gave his Son a gift, a love gift. He gave Jesus the disciples. Jesus mentions five times in his prayer in John 17 those "whom you have given me."[5] He also prays for those "who will believe in me through their word."[6] The Father gave the Son the Church

---

4. The Nicene Creed.

5. John 17:2; twice in 17:6; 17:9; 17:24.

6. John 17:20.

as his own possession. This image of the *gift* unites and unlocks the meaning in the three main Biblical images for the Church, the continuing community of Christ's disciples. In some places, Scripture speaks of the Church as the bride of Christ.[7] We, then, are the Father's gift of a bride for his Son. In other places, Scripture speaks of the Church as members of Christ's own body.[8] He is the head and we are the members, the parts of his body. Thus, the Church is the gift of the Father to the Son; of his body still being in the world, still enacting his will. In other places, the Church is spoken of as the temple of God, a house of worship built upon Jesus Christ as the foundation.[9] We are the gift of the Father to the Son of a beautiful, living temple where the Son may both dwell and be glorified. We are, in all these ways, the gift of the Father to the Son.

But we also are the gift of the Son to the Father. The Son came to us as Jesus Christ in order to find us when we were lost, to heal us when we were sick unto eternal death. He came to save us from our sin and misery. He came to live the obedience and love that we cannot live on our own. Then the Son gives all he has accomplished to us. He gives us his righteousness. He gives us his obedience. He gives us his Word. He gives us his eternal life. Then, after claiming and transforming us, Jesus offers the Church back to the Father:

> "I have manifested your name to the people whom you gave me out of the world ... For I have given them the words that you gave me, and they have received them and have come to know in truth that I came from you ... for they are yours."[10]

In other words, the Son seems to be saying, "You have given them to me, and I have taught them your Word, I have given them our love and life. So I offer these disciples back to you Father, as my offering of love to you. I have cleansed them and offer them now as spotless and pure through me, a gift to adorn your glory."

The third person of the Triune God, of course, has been active all along as well. The blessed Holy Spirit is the one who empowered the human Jesus in his obedience and love of his Father while on earth.[11]

---

7. Revelation 19:7; 21:2; Isaiah 54:5.

8. I Corinthians 12:12; Colossians 2:19.

9. Ephesians 2:20; I Peter 2:5.

10. John 17:7-9.

11. Luke 4:18.

The Spirit is the love by which Jesus could offer his life on the cross;[12] and the Spirit is the power of the resurrection.[13] This Holy Spirit is the gift of the Father through the Son to the Church.[14] God sends him to dwell in our hearts,[15] to be the glue between us and Christ. This understanding of the Holy Spirit as the gift from the Father through the Son to the Church works consistently through the three Biblical images of the Church. The Spirit is the mortar in the temple of God that holds us, the stones, together on the foundation. The Spirit is the sinews in the body that keep us, the members, attached to Christ our Head. The Spirit is the pledge of love, the ring on the finger of the Church who is the bride of Christ, that indicates we are promised and sealed for our union with our husband, the Lord Jesus Christ. The Spirit is the great Pentecostal gift of the Triune God to us.

But, as we might expect with this Triune gift-giving, other-glorifying, dynamically-loving God, we also are the Holy Spirit's gift to the Son and the Father. The Spirit labors in us to make us more and more like Christ.[16] He teaches us about Jesus, glorifying the ascended Christ in our midst.[17] He transforms us and empowers our ministry[18] as a love gift to the Father and the Son. The Spirit grows fruit within us,[19] endowing us with gifts to do Christ's work.[20] He seals our identity in Christ, guaranteeing that we will reach our goal[21] of life in the immediate presence of the Triune God.

So, we, the Church, are the *triple gift*. We are the gift of the Father to the Son. We are the gift of the Son to the Father. We are the gift of the Spirit to the Father and the Son. In this love of the persons of the Triune God giving us to one another, we are transformed. We were found by the Father who sent his Son to seek us when we were lost. We were called by the Spirit out of the darkness and into the light when he quickened us to new life. We were healed by the touch of the Son when we

---

12. Hebrews 9:14.

13. Romans 1:4.

14. Acts 2:33.

15. Galatians 4:6.

16. Romans 8:26-29.

17. John 16:13-16.

18. Acts 1:8.

19. Galatians 5:23.

20. I Corinthians 12:7.

21. Ephesians 1:13-14.

were broken and battered. We were forgiven in the name and by the loving work of the Father, Son and Holy Spirit. Our hard hearts were replaced with new hearts, with the Triune God who has taken up residence in us,[22] so that we may respond to the love of God and to one another.

The Church, then, is the creation of the Triune God, called into being as the three glorify one another. We have our life together always and only as recipients of grace that is not of our devising or deserving. We are the outworking of the divine love as it was and is expressed in the field of our humanity. In the terms of John 17, those who come to believe that Jesus was sent by the Father enter into the dynamic oneness of the love between the Father and the Son.[23] This faith recognizes Jesus as no mere man, but as the eternal Son of God come to us as a human being. Those whom the Spirit has quickened to life by creating faith in Christ Jesus as the Light of the world and the Lord of all, he also unites to Christ. They are one body, one bride, one living temple, joined together in Christ who is the head, the bridegroom, and the cornerstone of his Church.

Thus, the true Church is no human invention or institution:

- We are not a fellowship of people, in quest of the unknowable "divine," who have decided to band together along the way.

- Neither are we the association of those who discover they share a common guess about the mystery of God.

- We do not belong to one another by our own independent decision, but by the choosing of God – who called us together to see how he has made himself known in Christ.

- Moreover, our forming into particular denominations across the world neither constitutes nor breaks the universal fellowship of the Church. Associations between local churches form and reform as part of the ordering of our common life and of organizing for common mission. The fact that we do not relate to every other congregation in a community or nation does not break our bond in Christ. Nor does the fact that we are organizationally bound to certain congregations mean that such denominations always represent the true Church of Christ.

The nature of the Church is deeper than the human organization of

---

22. John 14:23.

23. John 17:8; 20-23; 25.

congregations. The Church is the fellowship of those given to the Son by the Father and to the Father by the Son in the loving bonds of the Holy Spirit. Participation in the Church is marked not by polity and property, but by right confession, sealed in the sacraments of Baptism and the Lord's Supper. It is expressed through visible, sacrificial love for another and robust mission to the world with the news of the Gospel.

Chapter Three

THE PEACE OF THE CHURCH

The peace of the Church is participating in the peace of Jesus; i.e., abiding in the victory of Jesus over the world, and being taken up into his story among us.

With the Trinitarian basis of our life in Christ established, the definitions of the ordination vow categories of "the peace, unity and purity of the church" follow readily. In this section, we consider the peace of the Church as a gift of the Triune God that results from being united in Christ.

Just before he began his prayer for the Church, Jesus concluded his teaching by saying, "I have said these things to you, that in me you may have peace. In the world you will have tribulation. But take heart, I have overcome the world."[1] Peace resides in Jesus. Tribulation issues from the world. The peace of Christ and the affliction of the world are set in contrast to one another. We cannot understand the peace of the Church without recognizing our enduring conflict with the world.

We know that God so loved the world that he gave his only begotten Son. The world as God's created humanity is the object of his seeking, searching love. But the world also is understood in Scripture as the whole system of resistance to the rule of the Triune God. The world is humanity's self-assertion of independence from anything higher than itself. It is our attempt to organize life in such a way that we control it. The world represents all the ways we desire to be our own gods, to place humanity at the center of existence. The world is humanity's system of trying to be sufficient on our own.

---

1. John 16:33.

In this world, spirituality is preferred to theology, since spirituality is what *I* choose for myself, the way *I* manage the mystery beyond me. The theological conviction that there is a God with a definite will and a known nature who makes an actual claim on us is considered by many to be a horrible infringement on our human rights. The world that desires to be self-determinate simply refuses Jesus' claim to be the Way, the Truth, and the Life. Such a Jesus would displace our egos on the throne of life, and that is not acceptable to the world.

In this way, the world is in conflict with the Church, which is the creation – and the servant – of the Triune God. The Church must accept the ever-present reality of this conflict. We may not evade it if we are to be faithful. Being engaged with the world is our mission.[2] We are locked in a struggle with the world for the sake of its salvation. If we avoid offending the world by quieting our witness to Jesus, we immediately become of no use to the very people whom God loves. Conversely, if we flee from engaging the world altogether, refusing the friction of the encounter while we stay in our church cloisters, we become of no use to the people for whom God died. The great Reformed missionary and theologian, Lesslie Newbigin, has written:

> The world does not know God. This contrast between knowing and not knowing God has to be stated with absolute clarity. Not to state it, to be silent about it, would be collusion with the power of the lie which rules the world. In a world which is organized around the self and seeks its own glory, the statement "I know God" will be seen as an outrageous piece of self-glorification. Agnosticism will be seen as a proper modesty. But this modesty does not provide any way of escape from the world which is centered in the self. Its genial tolerance ends abruptly in the face of a claim that God has actually revealed himself in the flesh and blood of the man Jesus. This claim will appear as a shocking assault upon the sovereignty of the autonomous reason and conscience.[3]

We are witnesses that the Light has come into the world of darkness. The love of God has been revealed in the sending of his Son Jesus to save us. This is the way God is. It is the most wonderful news ever reported. Some, though, see this as offensive because the truth of it knocks away every other prop that attempts to explain the reason why we are here and the purpose of human life. The world prefers to remain

---

2. John 17:15-18.

3. Newbigin, Lesslie; *The Light Has Come* (Grand Rapids, Mich.; William B. Eerdmans; 1984); p. 115.

agnostic so that the self remains in control. Choosing to attempt self-sufficiency, however, actually gives us no possibility of ever escaping from the prison of self-absorption and futility. We need an action from beyond to get us out of ourselves. God through the truth of Jesus Christ offers the way of freedom, even as this very grace evokes resistance from the world.

Thus, the peace of Jesus does not protect us from conflict. Our peace is not based on tranquil circumstances. It is found in the life of Jesus, who said:

> "Peace I leave with you; my peace I give to you. Not as the world gives do I give to you. Let not your hearts be troubled, neither let them be afraid. You heard me say to you, 'I am going away, and I will come to you.' If you loved me, you would have rejoiced, because I am going to the Father."[4]

Jesus' peace involves the history of his arrivals and departures in our midst:

- The eternal Son came to us as the Word became flesh and dwelt among us, full of grace and truth.[5] He entered our history; he took a place in the real world of dust and swiftly passing time;

- After the years of his wonderful ministry, Jesus departed from his disciples in his atoning death on the cross;

- Only to return three days later in bodily resurrection glory, alive again in the self-same body in which he was crucified, though now glorified, transformed and fitted for heaven;

- Then, at his ascension, Jesus – still in our flesh – departed again. Returning to his Father's right hand, he has sent us the Holy Spirit, who provides the inner assurance that;

- One day this same Jesus will arrive again in the world, drawing to a close this age and opening the eternity of our glorification, when his Church will dwell in the immediate presence of the Tri-une God.

Our peace, then, is based on the past, present and future victory of Jesus. Such peace is closely linked with our joy. Jesus, speaking about his impending arrest and crucifixion, said, "Truly, truly I say to you, you will weep and lament, but the world will rejoice. You will be sorrowful,

---

4.   John 14:27-28

5.   John 1:14.

but your sorrow will turn to joy ... you have sorrow now, but I will see you again, and your hearts will rejoice, and no one will take your joy from you."[6] The peace and joy of the Church are as indestructible as the continuing resurrection life of Jesus! The world did its worst to Jesus, but failed to stop him. The world can do nothing more to Christ's Church than it did to our Lord. Our present conflict or suffering cannot last indefinitely. Jesus' imminent return exposes all current worldly power and ecclesiastical organization as merely imperfect and provisional. Hence, our peace is anchored solely in Christ's victorious life.

This is why it is absolutely essential that the Church keep the entire story of Jesus ever before us. We must not allow the Gospel to be collapsed in any way that makes Jesus less or other than the eternal Son of God come to us in time as a human being, reigning now at the Father's right hand, and returning in glory. This means avoiding a whole series of wrong turns in our theology:

Jesus' history among us is not mere religious mythology invented by the Church. The events of incarnation, crucifixion, resurrection and ascension were real happenings in the real world, to be received truly by us through a plain reading of Holy Scripture.

Jesus may not be reduced to a collection of teachings. Jesus was not merely a man who provided a good example for us to follow. His words and actions were the words and actions of the one true God in our midst.

Nor may Jesus be considered a mere man who accessed the presence of God within him in a unique way. He was not a man in touch with some Christ-principle, nor a man who happened to be most favored by God because of his spirituality and ethics. He was, and is, Christ the Lord.

Jesus is not a partial revelation of God among other valid revelations, nor even the best glimpse of the mystery that can never be known. There is not more to the Christ than we meet in Jesus. There is no God behind the back of Jesus Christ.[7]

To say all this positively: to see Jesus is to see the Father.[8] Jesus is the

---

6. John 16:20, 22.

7. This concept, of Luthean/Barthian origin and oft asserted by Presbyterian theologian Thomas Torrance, assures us that, in encountering Jesus, we are encountering the one true, Triune God as he is in himself. There is not more of God hiding somewhere else in the sense that God would turn out to be something other than he appears to be in Christ Jesus our Lord.

8. John 14:9.

mystery of God made known, "in whom are hidden all the treasures of wisdom and knowledge."[9] He is the eternal Son of God himself come among us. This Jesus has passed victoriously through death to carry our humanity to the right hand of the Father. There he remains as our advocate and brother until he returns again to bring all things visibly under his rule. He prepares a place for us[10] and desires that we will be with him always. Our future is in glory with Jesus.

This is our peace amidst the conflict of the world and the last rages of the powers of death and evil. The Church knows that in Christ, at the deepest level of reality, all is well. That confidence, in the present and for the future, is the basis for being able to lay aside grievances over non-essentials. Because our true, eternal lives are kept in Christ, we have the freedom to be wronged and not seek revenge, to be disrespected and not be compelled to save face, to forgive rather than to bear grudges. We bear with one another not because we in ourselves have such gracious love, but because the Church knows how Christ has borne with his Church – enough to lay down his life and secure her eternal felicity. The peace of the Church is founded on our being taken into the unique, continuing, and saving life-story of our Lord Jesus Christ.

9.   Colossians 2:3.

10. John 14:2; 17:24.

Chapter Four

THE PURITY OF THE CHURCH

Submission in faith and life, confession and mission to the authority of the only true God who has sent Jesus Christ is the primary basis for the purity of the Church.

Our yearning for the peace of the world – the absence of conflict – can threaten the purity of the Church. We flirt with compromise in vain attempts to promote calm. We acquiesce to facets of the world's agenda, allowing them to invade the life of the Church in the hope that we will be better received by the world we seek to reach. As we engage our world, we are tempted to become like the world.

Jesus did not pray that the Church would be spared from the risk of this possibility. He sent us into engagement with the world. He prayed that, while enacting our mission, we would be kept *in* the name of his Holy Father and, thus, kept safe *from* the evil one.[1] We hear afresh Jesus' words, in today's denominational context, as the prayer that the church will not collapse her full telling of his story under contemporary pressure to soften our "edges." Indeed, we need a mighty work of God to keep us from compromising the church's borders in a culture where the very presence of moral or theological boundaries is considered taboo.

The stakes are high. If we falter in our witness as the Church of Christ in order to offer a more comfortable word in the short term, we ultimately end up being cruel to those who do not yet know Jesus. Speaking a language that does not offend the world, we fail to offer anything that can save the world from its self-centered will to power and its

---

1. John 17:11, 15.

bent for destruction. *The purity of the Church is vital to the salvation of the world.*

We return to Newbigin again:

> When the Church is kept in the holy name of God, it has a final commitment which is outside the comprehension of the world. Without this radical otherworldliness, the Church has no serious business with the world. Archimedes said: "Give me a point outside the world for a fulcrum and I will move the world with a lever." If the Church does not rest on a point outside the world, it has no leverage with the world. All its tugging and straining is but a minor disturbance within the life of the world, and therefore it is still under the power of the evil one. The Church is marked off from the world by the fact that it has received and must witness to the word of God which is the truth and which thereby calls in question all the so-called axioms, absolutes, and self-evident propositions which are the stock-in-trade of the world's life. It has to bear witness to the weakness and folly of a crucified messiah as the power and wisdom by which the world exists, is sustained, and will be judged. To accept this means to accept the overturning of the accepted wisdom of the world. It is therefore not a human possibility; it is a gift of God, a miracle, a new birth from above. Between the Church and the world, therefore, lies the boundary line which is called "conversion," and if the Church ignores this, it falls into the power of the evil one.[2]

The issue of the purity of the Church within the denomination of the PC(USA) concerns our accommodation to the world by adapting the theological assumptions and the ethical practices of the society around us. *Bluntly, the pressing danger is that the denomination is increasingly dissolving into the prevailing culture.* We too frequently adapt ourselves to the world rather than engaging the world from a place outside of its values and ambitions. If this continues, our denomination will no longer partake of the Church of Jesus Christ. We will have lost our saltiness[3] and hidden our light under a bushel. We will be irrelevant both to the world and the Church. We will be useless.

The purity of the Church requires locating our life outside the world system. It requires anchoring our denomination in the truth. Identifying his role before the Father, Jesus prayed, "… since you have given him authority over all flesh, to give eternal life to all whom you have given

---

2.   Newbigin; *The Light Has Come*; op. cit.; p. 235.

3.   In the Sermon on the Mount (Matthew 5:13), Jesus said, "You are the salt of the earth, but if the salt has lost its taste, how shall its saltiness be restored? It is no longer good for anything except to be thrown out and trampled under people's feet."

him. And this is eternal life, that they know you, the only true God, and Jesus Christ whom you have sent."[4] In unambiguous language, Jesus acknowledged his Father as the one and only, the sole, true God. He confirmed the witness at the heart of the Torah "that the LORD is God; there is no other besides him."[5] Indeed, "All the gods of the peoples are worthless idols,"[6] and "Thus says the LORD ... besides me there is no god."[7] The people of the God of Israel have never been, and never could be, polytheistic about God, as if he could be one of many gods. Nor could they be pluralistic in their confession, as if the LORD God could be known in many ways and guises. Our God is "jealous" for his people to acknowledge the truth of his sole Lordship. In this way, we will be able to offer the world its only hope for life – through entering a relationship with the one true God, the Triune God of love.

Further on, Jesus prayed:

> "I do not ask that you take them out of the world, but that you keep them from the evil one. They are not of the world, just as I am not of the world. Sanctify them in the truth; your word is truth. As you sent me into the world, so I have sent them into the world. And for their sake I consecrate myself, that they also may be sanctified in truth."[8]

Jesus desired that we, his Church, be set apart and made holy by the truth. He then affirmed that the Father's *word* is truth. How are we to understand this? Jesus himself is the Word of God[9] and he is the truth.[10] But the word of God written, Holy Scripture, also is truth.[11] The language of revelation speaks truly. The Triune God addresses us in Scripture in words we can grasp so that we truly know him. Jesus consecrated himself to his Father through his obedience to the Scriptures and in the obedience that led to the cross. He consecrated himself in order that we, his Church, also might be made holy in the truth.

Jesus gave his life that we might know that he himself is the fulfillment of the Old Testament Scriptures and the very truth to which the

---

4. John 17:3.
5. Deuteronomy 4:35.
6. Psalm 96:5.
7. Isaiah 44:6.
8. John 17:15-19.
9. John 1:14.
10. John 14:6.
11. John 17:17.

New Testament bears witness. Through Jesus, the Holy Scriptures have not lost, but actually gained, authority. Jesus reveals their deepest meaning and confirms their truth by his actions. Further, the record of his words and actions in the gospels, and the inspired witness to the meaning of Christ's presence among us in the Acts, the Epistles and the Revelation now take their place as Holy Scripture through which the Triune God addresses us. In his prayer, Jesus asked that his Church might be conformed to the truth of his Father's *word*. This means he desired that we be made more and more like himself, in accordance with the Scriptures, and so gathered ever deeper into his fellowship with the Father.

Thus, the Church is not without knowledge. Our purity requires this right knowledge. It is not arrogant to confess the truth. On the contrary, the greatest arrogance would be to fail to consecrate ourselves to the truth that has been revealed in Jesus. To say that we cannot know the truth is to insult God's ability to make himself known to his creatures. To imply that we know better how to live than the revealed word describes is sheer hubris.

At infinite cost, the Triune God has made himself known in a way that humanity can apprehend. We know, of course, that God cannot be *comprehended* by finite human minds still under the influence of sin and a sinful world. That is to say, not *everything* about God can be known. Yet, the Church always and everywhere has confessed that what can be known about God can be known *truly*. Moreover, what needs to be known about God in order to know him personally, to enter into the salvation of eternal life in Christ, can be *apprehended* by those to whom faith is given. Through Jesus Christ, we truly know the Triune God.

Deuteronomy 29:29 affirms that, "The secret things belong to the LORD our God. But what has been revealed belongs to us and to our children forever, that we may do all the words of this law." The revelation of the Triune God is the precious gift to the Church. We have been given this truth that we might know joy, and also that we might invite the world into the joy of this truth.

Jesus sent us as he himself was sent. The very mission of the Church is bound up in its purity, for the purity of the Church involves receiving and consecrating ourselves to the truth of Jesus and his word. We both preserve and pass on "the faith that was once for all delivered to the saints."[12]

Christian faith has *content*. This content may be identified in Scripture and throughout the centuries of faithful witness to the truth. We are

---

12. Jude 3.

not free to change either the story or the meaning of the words of the story. To say that Jesus Christ is Lord is to say that he is the truth whom every person has to acknowledge. To know Jesus truly is to know the one true God who is Father, Son and Holy Spirit. This God has made his will for our ethics and our mission known in Holy Scripture.

The evil one is the father of lies; the world lives under his deception that life may be found elsewhere than in Christ and his word. But we know that Jesus Christ is *the* truth. The purity of the Church means consecration to the truth once revealed regardless of any conflict, with the world or with one another, that it might create.

Chapter Five

THE UNITY OF THE CHURCH

Shared consecration to the truth of Jesus and his oneness with the Father is what enables our experience of the unity in Christ given to the Church.

A s Jesus turned his attention in prayer to those who would become believers through the centuries, he said, "I do not ask for these only, but also for those who will believe in me through their word, that they may all be one, just as you, Father, are in me, and I in you, that they also may be in us, so that the world may believe that you have sent me."[1]

The unity of the Church is the participation in the oneness of the Father and the Son in the Spirit. The mutual indwelling of the three persons has opened out to include us through the incarnation and redemptive work of the Son. As noted earlier, the Father has loved the Son utterly, perfectly and joyfully through eternity. And the Son has loved the Father, so much so that they may be said to be "in" one another. Each has his life in and through the other.

In the fullness of time, this love opened out to include us. The love story of the Father and the Son was enacted on the stage of our world. We were gathered up into that story because Jesus agreed to be united to our humanity. Coming among us, Jesus is the meeting place between us and the Father. Jesus is the matrix for the life of his Church. So he prayed, "I in them, and you in me, that they may be perfectly one."[2] We, individually and together, find the meaning of our existence inside the

---

1. John 17:20-21.
2. John 17:23.

love of the Father, the Son and the Spirit. *As each of us is located by faith within the life of God, we find a magnificent oneness with one another.*

The unity of the church, then, is not based on our being alike in outward forms such as our style of worship or polity. Neither do our proclamations of unity amidst diversity make us one. Unity is not based on us at all. The oneness of believers has its basis in the oneness of the Triune God, which, in Jesus, has opened out to include us. The Church is the fellowship of those who have been chosen and called to be members of Christ. United to him, we are joined to the Triune life of God. Thus, *in union with Christ*, we have our union with each other.

Yet, our response is crucial. Within this act of the Triune God to unite us to himself in Christ, we each make our response of faith and obedience. Thus, we are linked in the depths to all who answer the same calling. So, we expand our definition to conclude that the Church is the fellowship of those who have been chosen *and* called and who have replied with the faith that gives over the whole self to this choosing and calling Triune God of grace. We hear Jesus' summons and obey. We consent to take up our cross and follow him,[3] submitting our personal autonomy to his authority. The unconditional free grace of God's calling dissolves all claim of merit on our part. While this grace relieves us of the need to earn a place in this wondrous life of God, it nevertheless is absolutely demanding. The grace in our call to be joined to the Triune God incinerates any shred of self-assertion we might desire to retain. We are prevented from conceiving of God according to our will or wish. So, the unity in the Church is based not only on a shared calling, but also on sharing a complete consecration to the God who invites us into his Triune life. Our oneness is realized in daily experience through our mutual acceptance of Christ's claim on us.

Further, in Jesus' prayer, we see an inseparable link *between the unity of the Church and our witness to the world*. He prays a second time for our oneness in order that "the world may know that you sent me and loved them even as you love me."[4] Our unity will be the visible sign by which the Spirit draws others to believe. When the world sees the communion of those who have fellowship with the Father and the Son in the Spirit, the world realizes that Jesus was not merely a man, but the one sent from the Father. Those trapped in the darkness see the Light of the

---

3.   Mark 8:34.

4.   John 17:23.

world by beholding the unity of the Church. The mystical communion of believers with their Lord draws lonely and wandering people to Christ.

The connection between unity and witness explains why the struggle within our denomination matters so much, even though our institutional expression of the Body of Christ is rather numerically insignificant compared to the worldwide Church. A fragmented and fighting denomination portrays a contentious bride, a sick body, and an unstable, crumbling temple. People want no part of it. What meager peace and pleasure can be found in the world without God appears more attractive than our dysfunction. Moreover, our sickness can be contagious. Our disunity threatens to infect others. The PC(USA), for the sake of the world and the world Church, must recover its unity.

How? How do we reach a visible expression of unity based on the purity, the peace and the nature of the Church as expressed in Scripture and affirmed by the Church through the ages?

First, we must avoid some obvious traps. Making our unity in Christ visible again is not achieved by falling for the deception in such common half-truths as:

Unity means we must accept people with whom we differ, even people whom we dislike.

The truth in that statement accords with Scripture's encouragement that we be "eager to maintain the unity of the Spirit in the bond of peace."[5] We respond to the call, "Let each of you look not only to his own interests, but also to the interest of others."[6] We want to dress in "compassion, kindness, humility, meekness, and patience, bearing with one another and, if one has a complaint against another, forgiving each other."[7] The Christian strives to love all people, even the ones to whom we are not naturally drawn.

The error in that statement occurs, however, when it is used to enforce the acceptance of heretical beliefs and sinful behavior. The same one who urged us to "love one another, for love is from God,"[8] just six verses earlier commanded us to "test the spirits." He declared that, "Every spirit that does not confess Jesus is not from God. This is the

---

5. Ephesians 4:3.

6. Philippians 2:4.

7. Colossians 3:12-13.

8. I John 4:7.

spirit of the antichrist."[9] Love does not mean taking sin and error within the bosom of the Church; rather, the Church corrects errors in the knowledge of God and exercises discipline over sinful behavior.

"They" label as heretics anyone who does not agree with them, anyone who does not accept their narrow, fundamentalist expression of faith.

The truth in that statement exposes the sad reality that, in the past, Christians have wounded each other over non-essential elements of the faith. We each can become prone to emphasizing our favorite doctrines or raising to primacy our favorite Scriptural images. We can make legalistic claims, such as the use of alcohol and understandings of eschatology, in those areas that call for Christian freedom.

The error in such a statement, however, is the assumption that the essentials of Christian belief cannot be known, as if Scripture were not clear in matters related to salvation. Even more pernicious is the practice of re-interpreting words so that their historical meanings are vacated. Thus, as we have seen, the form of ancient and orthodox confession is maintained while the substance is denied – as if the words of Scripture and our confessions did not have content that has been agreed upon through the centuries and across cultures. The corollary to this reinterpretation are the labels hastily plastered on those who are historically orthodox – phrases such as rigid, right-wing, fundamentalist, arrogant, strident and extremist – so that the clarity of Biblical truth and Christian witness is de-legitimized. The unity of the Church is not served but, rather, is compromised when heterodoxy claims the center and turns against historic orthodoxy.

What matters most is that we all just get along.

This statement evokes a lovely passage in Romans 12. Paul writes, "Live in harmony with one another. Do not be haughty, but associate with the lowly. Never be conceited. Repay no one evil for evil, but give thought to what is honorable in the sight of all. If possible, so far as it depends on you, live peaceably with all."[10] Love strives for peace, even at the expense of one's own interests. Few fights are worth the energy and the cost of the conflict.

Some fights, however, are necessary. The Church may not accede to the demand, "You must love me without challenge to my beliefs lest you be guilty of dividing the Church. You must not discipline my behavior

---

9. I John 4:3.

10. Romans 12:16-19.

lest you be guilty of creating schism." The raising of indiscriminate peace as the highest value has been used to threaten the Church into a tolerance of what the Church never has and never can tolerate. Living in harmony, though, does not mean forcing the Church to call sin acceptable, nor to bless willful theological error in the essentials as being permissible under the law of love. Discipline is a vital part of the unity of the Church, for unity is only in Christ. Without consecration to the truth, there is no unity – only a false peace.

We must not impose our Western, middle-class values on others.

The truth in that statement convicts Christians of conflating their culture with the Gospel. We too easily can equate the suburban good life in America with the fruits of sanctification. Matters of dress, family customs, the societal economy, and even the form of our government can have a wide variety of expression and still fall within Biblical parameters.

The error in the statement is in equating Biblical morality with a Western way of life in such a way that church discipline or even the proclamation of Scriptural ethics is considered a form of cultural imperialism. In reality, our morality as Christians was revealed first to a people who only recently had been freed from four centuries of slavery. They had wandered for 40 years in the wilderness of the Middle East. Their culture and mentality did not resemble middle-class America. Moreover, our Gospel – and its imperatives – was not received first by the dominant social class, but by those to whom Paul said, "Not many of you were wise according to worldly standards, not many were powerful, not many were of noble birth."[11] The ethics for living revealed by the Triune God have ever been in contrast to, and in conflict with, the way the world arranges its quest for a self-sufficient "good life," independent of God.

As the world has come within the borders of the Church, our unity has been strained. We do not easily give up our desire to create God in our own image and arrange life according to our instincts. Thus, the Church – and, in particular, our denomination – has been conflicted. *Unity, however, cannot be restored simply by embracing an ever-widening, and even contradictory, array of beliefs and practices.* We must not yield to the temptation of permitting theological innovations and aberrations from Christian practice to be tolerated and blessed in the name of Christian unity. Down that path, as noted earlier, lies the dissolution of

---

11. I Corinthians 1:26.

the denomination into the world, with the resulting compromise of mission and the irrelevance of purpose.

The unity that has been given to the Church is discovered by the consecration of her members to the truth of Christ. The story of Jesus being sent from the Father summons us to a belief that is life-altering. At the beginning of his ministry, Jesus declared simply, "The time is fulfilled, and the kingdom of God is at hand; repent and believe in the gospel."[12] Repentance means a change of mind that leads to a change of life. It is a new way of seeing the world that results in a new way of living. Hence, we are called to die to the old way of seeing the world. In fact, we are called to refuse the world's quest to live independently from God. *We are summoned to bend the knee to the way God has made himself known.* We consecrate ourselves to the truth. As we believe, we undergo a kind of death. We are converted from the agenda of the world to the will of God. None of us comes naturally to such consecration. Such faith is a gift of the Spirit, who comes from above and remakes us completely – a gift that we dare not refuse in preference for our own agenda; rather, we receive it humbly, eagerly, worshipfully.

This shared repentance and common consecration to the truth of Christ, in our believing and in our living, fosters our experience of oneness in Christ. To the degree to which we abandon ourselves to the truth of the Father and the Son revealed in Scripture, we will know communion with fellow Christians who also follow Christ with reckless abandon. To the degree to which we continue to live half-committed to the world's agenda, our fellowship will be shallow, more perfunctory than realized. To the degree to which we stubbornly maintain our independence of will, thought and action, we distance ourselves from the mystical union of the Body. Church unity cannot be contrived; rather, our unity emerges out of our shared communion with the Triune God of love. Thus, the Church of Jesus Christ is the fellowship of broken wills, cracked-open hearts, bowed heads, bended knees, and submitted minds.

Once this clarity of vision is recovered, we then realize the sharp disjunction between the Biblical and orthodox theological understanding of the peace, unity and purity of the Church and the present reality in which the Presbyterian Church (USA) exists.

---

12. Mark 1:15.

Chapter Six

THE ALIEN ATMOSPHERE
OUR DENOMINATION BREATHES

The Presbyterian Church (USA) must be awakened from the spell of an atmosphere that has become normal for our times but is, in reality, alien and hostile to the Gospel.

One of the most destructive ideas in our current conflict is that because different interpretations of Scripture and Christian tradition exist, no definitive interpretation in matters of controversy is possible. The argument goes, "We just see it a different way. We're all faithful Christians. It's just a matter of interpretation. Remember, our Constitution says that people of good conscience may differ. So, let's avoid getting polarized over these issues." This embracing of "differences" dismisses the very heart of being confessional Christians, which is the declaration of what is so and not otherwise. Today, everyone may be – or even must be – right. No one can be wrong, so the distinction between truth and error, good and evil, must not be made.

The New Testament worldview was quite different. As the Church proclaimed the Gospel beyond Judaism to the Gentile world, strong distinctions were made between pagan culture and a new life in Christ. Paul, then, could praise the Thessalonians because "you turned to God from idols to serve the living and true God."[1] Thus, clear direction could be given concerning what, today, is one of the presenting problems in our denomination:

"For this is the will of God, your sanctification: that you abstain from

---

1. I Thessalonians 1:9.

sexual immorality; that each of you know how to control his own body in holiness and honor, not in the passion of lust like the Gentiles who do not know God; that no one transgress and wrong his brother in this matter, because the Lord is an avenger in all these things... For God has not called us to impurity, but in holiness. Therefore whoever disregards this, disregards not man but God, who gives his Holy Spirit to you."[2]

Holiness of behavior for those who have come to know Christ is not optional. In fact, now knowing the God of truth, the peril of disregarding his word appears to be all the greater. Paul later makes the contrast as sharp as possible by declaring, "For you are all children of light, children of the day. We are not of the night or of the darkness."[3]

Peter employs the same metaphor when he writes of how we are called to "proclaim the excellencies of him who called you out of darkness and into his marvelous light."[4] Because we have been led out of the darkness in which the world lives, Peter urges us "as sojourners and exiles to abstain from the passions of the flesh, which wage war against the soul. Keep your conduct among the Gentiles honorable...."[5] Our calling in Christ makes us strangers in the world. Our homeland is now heaven, so that we experience life here as exiles, as people who never can be at home because we belong to another land, though we serve this "foreign" world with the love of the Gospel.

The "air" of this world is not the atmosphere of our true country. So, when the Church gathers, we partake of an atmosphere quite different from the world. We savor together the scent of what it will be like to arrive home. We are meant to breathe the air of heaven as the Scriptures are rightly proclaimed, the Sacraments celebrated and the Triune God worshipped in Spirit and in truth. Should the Church get confused and import the values of the world into its gathered life, however, we begin to breathe an alien, poisonous atmosphere. Though out in the world we cannot help but make our way among those who hold destructive values and effuse a hostile ideology, within the gathered Church there should be the respite of light and truth. When the world's air seeps into the Church on its Sabbath rest, we are weakened for our service. Our very identity becomes confused.

---

2. I Thessalonians 4:3-8.

3. I Thessalonians 5:5.

4. I Peter 2:9.

5. I Peter 2:11-12.

There is no lack of clarity, for example, regarding sexual matters in the Scriptures. Romans 1 describes homosexual passions and practice as one of the clearest expressions of what results when the truth of God is exchanged for a lie."[6] In I Corinthians, Paul defines *porneia*, the word used for sexual immorality in general, as including heterosexual adultery as well as both the passive and active participants in homosexuality.[7] Historically orthodox churches have done the work in scholarship on this issue to expose all reinterpretations of Biblical teaching as being unsustainable.[8] These matters are so settled that, for faithful Christians, "sexual immorality and all impurity and covetousness *must not even be named among you*, as is proper among saints."[9] Concordantly, Paul was outraged at the arrogance of the Corinthians, who allowed incestuous sexual immorality among them of "a kind that is not tolerated even among pagans."[10]

The normal atmosphere in the Church, then, should be the consistent expectation of sexual holiness as Christians are brought more and more into conformity to Christ by the sanctifying power of the Spirit. Sinful behavior is to be met with loving discipline. The goal is the gentle restoration of brothers and sisters, while being aware that any of us is prone to sin.[11] Ultimately, unrepentant sin must be answered with the removal of the one who will not cease so that the peace, purity and unity of the Church may be preserved.[12] Though the nuances of such discipline are beyond our scope, we note that the Biblical expectation is not the tolerance of behavior that is clearly and persistently sinful, but discipline that leads to the realignment with the truth.

In the Presbyterian Church (USA) today, however, we breathe a decidedly different air. In contrast to the consecration to Christ and his

---

6. Romans 1:25-27.

7. I Corinthians 6:9.

8. Gagnon, Robert; *The Bible and Homosexual Practice* (Nashville, Tenn.; Abingdon Press; 2001). In this book and subsequent articles, Gagnon has sustained the traditional orthodox view of sexual ethics as being, indeed, the correct interpretation of Scriptural teaching. His opponents now admit this and assert a new ethic by appealing not to what has been revealed in Scripture, but by appealing to new light from the Spirit that goes beyond Scripture (as if that were not a theological impossibility). See also Kenneth Bailey's work on I Corinthians.

9. Ephesians 5:3. Emphasis added.

10. I Corinthians 5:2-3.

11. Galatians 6:1.

12. I Corinthians 5:2.

word that creates the experience of unity, the PCUSA has been asked to consecrate itself and its historic witness to the acceptance and even blessing of theology and practices alien to the Church. Paul notes that the natural course of the world's assertion of independence against God leads people to affirm sin in all its destructiveness:

> "Though they know God's decree that those who practice such things deserve to die, they not only do them but give approval to those who practice them."[13]

Within our denomination, there are strong factions asserting approval to what Scripture clearly has condemned. The drumbeat of this demand for approval has been so persistent that we actually have ceded much ground. We have been breathing poisonous air for so long that we have come to believe it is normal. As a denomination, we have "walked, following the course of this world, following the prince of the power of the air, the spirit that is now at work in the sons of disobedience."[14]

This is a harsh claim. We test it by asking a series of questions: Has the culture of the United States been expressing Christian values in an increasing or decreasing way? Are we satisfied that our culture is caring for children, the elderly, the poor, and the hungry in a better way over the last decades? Do we find, as American culture is increasingly post-Christian, that the Presbyterian Church (USA) looks more sharply different than the culture in which we live? Or, rather, do we see evidence that the denomination consistently makes choices to mirror the culture? Do our recent innovations in doctrine and practice seem redemptively counter-cultural to American life? Or do they conform increasingly to the social pressures in our country?

In reality, there is a significant disconnect between our official theology and what Phillip Turner has termed our "working theology." The denomination's Constitution remains in congruence with historic orthodoxy and the witness of the Church around the world. But our practice, even our preaching and our teaching, has grown increasingly like the pluralistic culture of our nation. Our theology is less orthodox and more like what Turner calls "radical inclusion." In this view, the acceptance of all beliefs and behavior without qualification is the path to personal fulfillment and communal harmony and love. Such an inclusion, without the need for transformation, has replaced the historic understanding that healing and wholeness come not from changing the definition of sin,

---

13. Romans 1:32.

14. Ephesians 2:2.

but through Christ's grace-filled redemption of our lives from sin.[15]

Along a similar line, researchers Christian Smith and Melinda Lundquist have described the dominant American religion as "Moralistic Therapeutic Deism."[16] In this theology, God's chief interest is in our being kind to one another and being fulfilled in ourselves. God's main role is to help us if we have a problem in achieving the life we have chosen to pursue. The reality of sin, the need for redemption and the call to repentance and holiness seem not to be recognized. Today, the Presbyterian Church (USA) appears to be grievously affected by these alien theologies.

Our denomination is ill. We have come to believe that it is normal to live with what amounts to contradictory theologies (and, hence, contradictory ethics) within one expression of the Church. We do not realize how poisoned is the atmosphere in which we exist. The people of the world, even non-Christians, recognize our illness. They stay away from us. We are not replacing our losses. We are not retaining our young people. Whether this sickness is unto death or not remains to be seen, but time grows short. Now is the season to lift our heads and realize where we are. Now is the time to look beyond the American church culture to the Church of Jesus Christ expressed around the world. We have listened openly for decades to error and dangerous innovation. Now we must listen to our brothers and sisters in the Two-Thirds World who are crying out to us to repent while we yet can. The world Church names the corruption in the West. At great financial risk to their impoverished congregations, they call us back to the faith we once held. Does the denomination have the humility to listen?

The time has come for churches in the Presbyterian Church (USA) to step into the truth, even at the risk of persecution, and break the spell that is upon us. Though it causes discomfort, and even evokes anger, we must unmask what influences alien to the Gospel have become parts of the working theology of our denomination. Like ice-cold water, these 10 rhetorical questions splash us in the face:

1. How have we tolerated an outward confessional unity that is predicated on allowing multiple meanings of theological words – thus, changing the historic, universal meaning of these confessional

---

15. Turner, Phillip; "An Unworkable Theology," First Things; (June/July 2005); pp. 10-12.

16. Smith, Christian and Lundquist, Melinda; Soul Searching: The Religious and Spiritual Lives of American Teenagers; (Oxford University Press; New York; 2005).

words – in order to maintain the claim of being in the center of the faith?

2. How have we dared to call the everlasting sacrifice of the union of the eternal Son of God with our human flesh, at infinite cost to himself, to be one path among many paths? Under what authority have we turned from God's clear and final revelation of himself in Christ Jesus, calling any witness to that truth arrogant?

3. How could we trifle with the priceless gift of Jesus placing the name of his Father in our mouths and the Holy Spirit vocalizing that name on our tongues by trivializing "Father" as an optional metaphor and raising up inanimate objects and projections as worthy substitutes?

4. How could we ever call the taking of an unborn life a faithful choice? With every advance of the natural sciences affirming human life from conception, how could we give a hearing to the thought, let alone the action, of taking a human life from the womb to destroy it?

5. How could we contemplate that the physical merging of two people of the same gender could be a new thing of the Spirit; a step forward for humanity; acts that cannot be procreative and do not represent the completion of one through an "other" but, rather, bespeak a choice to remain in undifferentiated sameness? How do we contemplate calling such brokenness whole?

6. How could the church in America become so enamored with the idols of wealth, worldly power and entertainment that we constantly allow ourselves to be fed and shaped by an alien worldview? Thus, how have we come to see God as merely an optional spiritual accent on the "good life" that we compose for ourselves?

7. How could we idolize sports, activities and affluence so that, for all our collective wealth and leisure, we have little time to care for the poor and the lost, or to form our young people in Christ; little energy for engaging in mission or leading our young people into mission; and little money left over to tithe and do the work of God's kingdom?

8. How could we decry same-sex activity without providing loving, mature, wise support for the transformation of those who are sexually broken or conflicted?

9. How is it possible that heterosexual sins of infidelity, pornogra-

phy, promiscuity, divorce and abusive or neglectful marriages continue to grow in the church?

10. How can we condemn abortion and euthanasia while failing to adopt unwanted children, care for the elderly, lay down our lives for the children in our communities, and restore elders to a place of dignity?

In allowing these questions to pinpoint the theology and behavior too often expressed in our denomination, we realize that in large part, as the PC(USA), we have lost our distinction from the culture and are irrelevant to the needs of a hurting, dying world. We have lost our confidence in Scripture and our clear witness to the single, saving Lordship of Jesus Christ. We have spent decades debating while failing to exercise loving, redemptive discipline.

The time has come to recall the deep, simple truths related to our present conflict:

- There is no God but the one revealed in Jesus Christ as Father, Son and Holy Spirit. All spiritual paths do not lead to the same place. Jesus Christ alone is Lord. "And there is salvation in no one else, for there is no other name under heaven given to men by which we must be saved."[17]

- Thus, we are not universalists. The Church is sent that the world may know the Father through the Son in the Spirit. The world, however, may decline this knowledge, but the consequences are everlasting. People can be lost. Thus, our witness must be urgent and our message clear.

- Homosexual behavior is sinful. The witness of Scripture on this issue is unequivocal and clear. We may not settle for sexual orientation to be the final, or even dominant, definition of someone's personhood. The Church may not isolate people in their brokenness by blessing what is wrong. That momentary acceptance ultimately is cruel, since it leaves others languishing in their sin and pain. Thus, we may not bless active homosexual behavior by declaring it not to be a barrier to the consecration of the self that is inherent in the sacrament of Baptism. We may not bless same-sex unions nor ordain practicing homosexuals to the ministry. In love, we must offer a better, more healing way.

- The lives of the unborn are precious to the Triune God of grace.

---

17. Acts 4:12.

We do not have the authority to make choices about their lives. The Church of Jesus Christ, from the earliest days, has stood clearly against abortion and on the side of life, in the name of the one who came to "the least of these."[18] Thus, abortion is not a faithful option for Christians but, instead, represents the holocaust of this generation. It leads to a devaluing of all people in our culture. It ultimately is cruel not only to the babies that are destroyed, but also to the mothers and fathers who made the deadly choice. Our silence in this matter is a blight upon the soul of the Church.

- The heterosexual sins in our promiscuous culture have invaded the Church and urgently must be addressed with calls to repentance and making available the resources for loving transformation. While we have focused on homosexuality in recent years, the vastly greater numbers of sexual sins and the resultant brokenness often have been passed over in silence.

In light of all the above, it is imperative that we robustly cultivate ministries that foster choices for life – including shelter, guidance and nurture for mothers and fathers in the case of unexpected or problem pregnancies; the promotion of adoption; and the strengthening of marriages and families. We must create communities characterized by listening, healing and Biblical, loving support for those struggling with same-sex attraction, with the after-effects of abortion, or with sexual brokenness in any form. We must bring to focus the transforming power of Christ in these lives. We must provide the concrete "Yes" of love to those who only have heard the "No" of our Biblical ethics.

The Presbyterian Church (USA) is wasting precious time and energy debating what is not debatable. The time for deliberating these issues has long been concluded. We will not give error an equal footing with the truth any longer. To do otherwise is to collude with the lies of the enemy of the Church. To do otherwise is to be cruel to those who are suffering in bondage to their sin. To proclaim less is to fail to offer the whole truth of Christ to a broken world.

---

18. Matthew 25:40.

Chapter Seven

A CALL TO FAITHFUL ACTION
FROM ACTS 15-16

The declaration of apostolic boundaries energizes the Church for mission and growth.

To a denomination that loses tens of thousands of members yearly, the words of Acts 16:5 offer a lovely vision: "So the churches were strengthened in the faith, and they increased in numbers daily." What caused such growth? Could it be ours again?

The vigorous life in the early churches flourished after the resolution of the conflict over circumcision. The assertion that the ancient mark of being part of the covenant community was essential to receiving the grace of Jesus Christ created "no small discussion and debate."[1] What was the relationship between keeping the Law and trusting in the salvation wrought through the life, death and resurrection of Jesus? The "Judaizers" wanted to add requirements to the Gospel. The matter was brought to the apostles and elders in Jerusalem. After much study and debate, the council concluded that salvation is in Christ alone.

The council then declared that while a ceremonial dimension to the Law had been fulfilled in the work of Christ, the Church was not without ethical imperatives. James concluded, "Therefore my judgment is that we should not trouble those of the Gentiles who turn to God, but should write to them to abstain from the things polluted by idols, and from sexual immorality, and from what has been strangled, and from blood."[2] The churches were to be free of ceremonial requirements that did not partake of the essentials of obedience. Those essentials were

---

1. Acts 15:2.
2. Acts 15:19-20.

given as the command to avoid what partakes of idolatry, to avoid *porneia* (all forms of sexual immorality including adultery, homosexuality and fornication), and to eschew what would be most offensive to Jews, the consuming of strangled animals or blood.

When a decision had been reached, the apostles sent out trusted disciples to deliver the message to the churches. They wrote a letter that was to be personally delivered to all the congregations. The contents will be instructive for the PC(USA):

> "Since we have heard that some persons have gone out from us and troubled you with words, unsettling your minds, although we gave them no instructions, it has seemed good to us, having come to one accord, to choose men and send them to you with our beloved Barnabas and Paul, men who have risked their lives for the sake of our Lord Jesus Christ. We have therefore sent Judas and Silas who themselves will tell you the same things by word of mouth. For it seemed good to the Holy Spirit and to us to lay on you no greater burden than these requirements: that you abstain from what has been sacrificed to idols, and from blood, and from what has been strangled, and from sexual immorality. If you keep yourselves from these things, you will do well. Farewell."[3]

So, the chosen messengers went off with the letter. In Antioch, they assembled the congregation and read the contents: "And when they had read it, they rejoiced because of its encouragement."[4] The clarity of teaching by the apostles created joy in the congregation. Settling the matter of the dispute with authoritative teaching released energy in the church. Moreover, the letter was followed with personal teaching by those who had been at the council: "And Judas and Silas, who were themselves prophets, encouraged and strengthened the brothers with many words."[5] The decrees were explained, and the congregation was connected to the rest of the Church.

In this context, we see how the vigorous growth in numbers and spirit occurred. "As they went on their way through the cities, they delivered to them for observance the decisions that had been reached by the apostles and elders who were in Jerusalem. So the churches were strengthened in the faith, and they increased in numbers daily."[6] The

---

3.   Acts 15:24-29.

4.   Acts 15:31.

5.   Acts 15:32.

6.   Acts 16:4-5.

messengers did not come to open a dialogue or engage in a debate. They came to deliver the apostolic teaching. *That clarity freed the churches for mission and growth.*

In our own context, we can imagine the effect of a clear witness to "the faith that was once for all delivered to the saints."[7] Congregations are straining under the yoke of alien ideas from our culture that have been introduced into the life of the American church. The innovations of the culture are a burden on the churches. Promising freedom from restraint, they actually are a form of bondage that keeps us from the truth of Christ, puts clamps on the mission of the Church, and places dampers on the Spirit's work. So, we yearn to hear a word from the apostles spoken to our present context. It might sound like this:

> Brothers and sisters, we have heard that certain people have gone out from us and troubled you with words, unsettling your minds, although we gave them no instructions. We want you to know that we have come to one accord on these matters.
>
> We do not want you to be burdened any longer with:
>
> • Worrying whether or not there is a God other than the God revealed in Jesus Christ, as if you had to be pluralists;
>
> • Concern whether the Scriptures mean what they say and say what they mean, as if you had to give them over to innovative "interpretations;"
>
> • Wondering if you must accommodate sexual immorality, including homosexuality, as normal or even a blessing from God;
>
> • Bearing the enforced silence of our complicity in the deaths of the unborn.
>
> Rather, we want to deliver to you the decision of the apostles, that you might have the freedom of these boundaries.
>
> So we sent you those who risked their lives for the Gospel.

People in Presbyterian churches from around the world witness to the power of declaring the teaching of the apostles. David Githii, moderator of the four-million member Presbyterian Church of East Africa, witnesses[8] to the price that has been paid because "the African church will never compromise," and the joy and growth resulting from such fidelity to the Scripture. Lugero Morais, general secretary of the Presbyterian Church of Brazil, witnesses to how new churches are being started

---

7. Jude 3.

8. These ministers spoke during a New Wineskins Convocation titled "Following Christ into the 21st Century" on June 15-18, 2005, in Edina, Minn.

almost daily in his country as the pure, simple Gospel is preached from leaders who believe evangelism is essential. Sameh Maurice, pastor of a 7,000-member congregation in Egypt, witnesses to how Muslims are risking their lives to become baptized as Christians because the beauty and truth of Christ Jesus is worth more than life itself.

And, so, we would see that these alien innovations in our denomination need trouble us no more. We will declare the truth. We no longer will accept error in the essentials as a difference of interpretation. The time has come to be the Church again in the Presbyterian Church (USA).

Chapter Eight

GOING TO DECLARE TRUTH

We call upon each individual and session embracing this work to go and bear witness to other individuals and sessions concerning the truth of the Gospel as it relates to the present context.

The apostles sent trustworthy messengers to go from congregation to congregation bearing witness to the truth and delivering their decrees. Personal interaction was crucial. I believe that the path forward in the Presbyterian Church (USA) similarly involves the person-to-person witness of those who hold to historic orthodoxy in theology and ethics. As we claim the clarity of the apostolic witness, we, too, are called to go to other congregations. This is a season for sessions to articulate those aspects of faith and practice that they understand to be essential. Then, we are called to move outward. We have a Gospel to share within our own denomination. If we do not go face to face, we will not have fulfilled our Christian obligation to encourage, warn, exhort and strengthen our brothers and sisters. Further, I believe that if we do not go personally, we will not be able to discern the next step in our life as a denomination.

Though the time to proclaim the Gospel always is right now, there is particularly urgency in our present context. In the summer of 2006, the General Assembly will be asked to make or to recommend decisions that will lead the Presbyterian Church (USA) into greater conformity with the world. The first desire of renewal leaders is that the assembly will reject such suggestions and joyfully uphold our historic witness. We labor to that end. But should the assembly make those decisions that further weaken our distinction from the world and our witness to the truth, the presbyteries and churches will have to wrestle over this pro-

posed new denominational landscape. We strive to prepare the churches
for such a struggle, even as we pray it does not come to pass. In this
season, then, we urge churches to act before the need for reaction arises.

I envision sessions studying the preceding pages of *Given and Sent
in One Love* as inspiration for articulating what is essential in our faith
and practice. Then, those same sessions will take the daring step of asking to visit the sessions of at least six other congregations. There is a
step-by-step guide on p. 145 for sessions willing to undertake this jour-
ney from articulating truth to bearing witness. We will go forward not to
condemn or to judge, but to bear witness to what we believe and have
come to know as the truth. We go to declare where we stand as congregations in the Presbyterian Church (USA) *before* the next crucial decisions are made. We go to describe the historic, yet fresh, vision for
faithfully being the Presbyterian Church once more.

It is essential that individuals and sessions profess that on the basic
questions of the person of Christ, Biblical authority and sexual ethics,
there is no further debate. The Church has spoken, consistently and
faithfully, across the centuries and throughout the globe. We no longer
will bear error as an acceptable alternative to truth. The 1978 General
Assembly's Authoritative Interpretation is an excellent, compassionate
and orthodox statement that we will not concede but, rather, will celebrate. Without it, the ordination standards of G.6-0106b in the *Book of
Order* of the Presbyterian Church (USA) may be gutted of their force by
revisionist interpretation. For us, the plain meaning of G.6-0106b is
foundational.

We call upon individuals and sessions to ask other individuals and
sessions if they may come to share their heart, share what is most basic
to their faith and life. We ask elders to go and bear witness to the truth.
We do not go to condemn, but to declare what we hold to be true. We go
to invite these other individuals and sessions to join us in standing for
the historic faith and witness of the Presbyterian Church and that it be
maintained in working reality, as well as in constitutional status. We go
to declare where our congregations will stand no matter what decisions
are made in the future by the denomination.

We have seen that the truth of Jesus Christ calls us to *repentance*.
Our unity is based on a shared consecration to Christ as he is revealed
in his word. Therefore, as we declare truth to our brothers and sisters,
we do so calling for repentance. This means we go with a spirit of
humility since we will confess not only the truth, but also our own
falling away from the truth in belief and practice. Then, on the basis of
the declaration of truth and our own confession of sin in the specific

areas where we have failed, we call for repentance. We pledge ourselves to repent of the ways in which we have sinned against the truth. And, so, we have grounds to call our sister congregations to join us in confessing and repenting where we have failed Christ's truth. We summon others with the declaration of truth, and model the confession and repentance to which God calls us. The particular form of repentance required of each church will differ. We will not name that form for our brothers and sisters. At the same time, however, we will not concede that, on these essential issues, there is more than one truth or even more than one way to see the truth. We will let the clarity of the truth shine forth even if it provokes hostility.

When these visits have been conducted, we will know what God calls us to do. We must care enough to go face to face. We must dare enough to proclaim truth without backing down. We must share enough so it is clear that the time of debating over essentials, dialoguing without reference to the truth, and entertaining the possibility of accepting error is over. The time of repentance is at hand.

We cannot say what response we will meet. Perhaps a great outpouring of the Holy Spirit will rouse the churches to embrace the truth and throw off the yoke of recent, erroneous innovations in theology and ethics. Perhaps we will encounter resistance and even persecution. Perhaps we will be met with indifference. Perhaps this institution of the Presbyterian Church (USA) cannot remain in its present form if the mission of the Gospel is not to be compromised. Those outcomes will sort themselves out. For the present, the results don't matter to the task at hand – we must go for the sake of our brothers and sisters. Then, and only then, will clarity be given about the next steps in this denomination.

Brothers and sisters, pray that the peace, purity and unity of the Church will fill our denomination, that Jesus Christ might be praised to the glory of God the Father in the power of the Holy Spirit. We long for the Presbyterian Church (USA) to again share boldly and truly in the one true Church of Jesus Christ, given in the eternal love of the Triune God, and sent into that world to bless the world.

Book Two

Gracious Act Gracious Response

The Character of the Church Under God's Redeeming Love

TABLE OF CONTENTS

Introduction

INVITATION

The 213th General Assembly (2001) acknowledged the growing discord and disunity within the Presbyterian Church (USA) and appointed the Theological Task Force on Peace, Unity and Purity to study the issues involved and lead the church into a better future. This group, comprised of members of vastly different theological perspectives that met for four years, endeavored to fulfill its mandate by accurately describing the situations within the church that are leading to our division and strife and to make recommendations for restoring and building the peace, unity and purity of the church. The initial covenant[1] created by the task force reflects a genuine integrity and Christian ethic. Their work and interrelationships have demonstrated and exhibited healthy dialogue and a model of Christian community.

Three years after its formation, the task force, in a preliminary report to the General Assembly, made the following recommendation:

> The Theological Task Force on Peace, Unity and Purity of the Church recommends that the 216th General Assembly (2004) encourage every presbytery to create intentional gatherings of Presbyterians of varied theological views to covenant together to discuss the affirmations in the task force's preliminary report, utilizing the resources being developed by the task force; and that sessions be encouraged to do the same.

This study is intended to be one means of practically and intentionally accepting this recommendation. Here we offer theological and Biblical reflections meant to provide additional understanding to the current conflicts with the Presbyterian Church (USA), suggest our theological

---

1. See Appendix 1 of the report of the Theological Task Force on Peace, Unity and Purity of the Presbyterian Church (USA) at www.pcusa.org/peaceunitypurity.

perspective, and make recommendations that we feel are faithful to both God and our theological tradition and necessary if the church is to know true peace, unity and purity.

We hold that theology matters and that peace, unity and purity, if they actually are to exist, must emerge from the truth; from the Gospel of Jesus Christ rightly understood, enjoyed and proclaimed; and from a true and accurate knowledge of God's will and work to bring genuine redemption and healing to the human race. There is no other way to peace, unity or purity. Such qualities are beyond mere mandate, hope or human endeavor. Rather, like the Gospel from which they come and to which they bear witness, these are gifts that come from proper understanding, reception and practice of the Gospel. It is not enough, therefore, to simply decree peace any more than one simply can pronounce or wish for purity. These are the fruit of genuine faith given as a divine gift to all who walk faithfully, obediently and intentionally with the Triune God.

It is, therefore, required of all who would seek the peace, unity and purity of the church to know and properly respond to the faith once and for all delivered to the saints.[2] With this in mind, and reflecting upon the primarily theological nature of the mandate placed upon the task force, we endeavor here to reflect upon the Biblical and theological issues involved and to suggest, in light of this, recommendations for the Presbyterian Church (USA) that may bring about our goal of peace, unity and purity. It is not our intention to merely proclaim or demand "peace, peace...," but to articulate the means, reasons and source of it being known and enjoyed.

We accept the invitation to study the issues currently tearing at the Presbyterian Church (USA), to reflect upon the theology of the church and its perspective of our current malaise, and, through this paper, enter into dialogue with the larger Church in the hope of providing understanding and promoting the peace, unity and purity of our church. We invite the larger Church to listen, reflect and respond to what we here set forth that we might move forward within the goals and aim of the 213th General Assembly and the Theological Task Force on Peace, Unity and Purity.

---

2. This very phrase from Jude 3 presumes that proper theological work, even as it is expanding and deepening, must have some continuity with the essential elements of the faith held across time.

Chapter One

THE TASK

The pursuit, maintenance and protection of peace, unity and purity is both essential and difficult. Essential because each is mandated and expected of the church in the Scriptures and our constitution. Essential because it manifests and reflects the eternal nature of the Triune God who exists as one being in three persons in perfect peace, unity and purity. The church is comprised of men and women who have been called from death to life, from sin to holiness, from the world into the body of Christ, for the purpose of revealing and manifesting in the created order God's grace and nature. Peace, unity and purity are essential and necessary characteristics of the church and, where they are blurred, the church's witness also is blurred and diminished. Where they are lost, the church ceases to be.

The difficulty in discovering the means and enjoying the benefits of peace, unity and purity, however, can be profound for the simple fact that, in a fallen and broken world, these carry in their relationship an inherent tension. What may facilitate unity may well damage or weaken purity; the pursuit of Biblical purity may limit peace.[1] This inherent tension makes equilibrium profoundly difficult to achieve and maintain. Most commonly, one or two of the required three rise to prominence while another is neglected; one is stressed and taught while the others are ignored. Anyone who seeks to study must understand and address this inherent tension and the point(s) of emphasis needed to provide or restore equilibrium. We may not claim success or the task accomplished where one or two are successfully achieved and the remaining weakened

---

1. As popularly or culturally understood. In fact, genuine purity will result in genuine peace and genuine unity. As an eschatological hope and reality, it will find real, but only partial, manifestation in the temporal order.

or lost. For these three are inextricably bound to one another and, in the end, the loss of one inevitably will lead to the loss of all and, thus, the life and witness of the church. To proclaim "peace, peace..." when there is no peace or to be satisfied with a unity isolated from any real understanding and practice of purity will suffer the loss of all three. Peace will flee where conscience is denied a voice. Unity requires genuine peace, not a cease-fire, if it is to be real.

Nor may we proclaim the task accomplished if we achieve a peace, unity or purity understood differently from that which the Scriptures and our Reformed theological tradition allow. Peace, for example, is a broadly held and readily understood concept and goal. Yet, rarely does the popular and cultural understanding of peace bear the weight and depth of meaning found in the Biblical word *shalom*. Peace, unity and purity lie beyond grasp or comprehension when the nature and definitions of each remain ambiguous or (synonymously, perhaps) culturally defined. Too often, the church has allowed cultural and popular understandings of such words to replace the Biblical and theological understandings. Or, worse, it intentionally has redefined them in order to express a particular polemic, philosophy or agenda. The end result is that words bearing a profound depth of meaning – peace, unity, purity, grace, forgiveness, etc. – have been rendered anemic and vapid. That this has occurred in the Presbyterian Church (USA) is obvious and easily illustrated: Within our denomination, the Biblical term unity effectively has been replaced with the far weaker *connectional*. Consequently, through years of use within the church, we became content with being connected – a political and institutional value – without knowing or experiencing Biblical unity. Many such examples abound. In recent years, words like grace, chastity, monogamy, commitment, faithfulness and purity all have undergone a semantic shift within the church and now express meanings that are disparate, inconsistent and confusing.

In our study of the pursuit and maintenance of peace, unity and purity, it is essential that we understand each from a Biblical and Reformed perspective. To replace *shalom* with tolerance, unity with connectionalism, and purity with personal choice is to have completely failed. To proclaim "peace, peace ..." when there is, in fact, no peace as Biblically understood is to strip the church of the concept and experience of real peace. To allow peace to mean nothing more than tolerance and the celebration of diversity is to deny the church and its members the opportunity of experiencing real *shalom*. In the end, there is no difference between using these words in isolation from the Biblical and theological meanings and not using them at all.

All who are ordained in the Presbyterian Church (USA) vow to maintain the peace, unity and purity of the church. But to make the promise and voice the words does not automatically mean any one or even all of these actually will become realities. Such qualities do not manifest themselves simply by wish or promise, since each is the fruit and consequence of the Gospel of Jesus Christ rightly proclaimed, believed and practiced. Like a canary in a mine, the breadth and vitality of these characteristics reveal the depth to which a people of God actually are living within and enjoying the Gospel. Their erosion or loss, on the other hand, is indicative of a far greater crisis. Tragically, the facts before us reveal that we are facing a lethal challenge: Our peace, unity and purity are dissolving as strife, disunity and license increasingly have come to characterize our corporate life. We are hemorrhaging members at a rate so fast that the Presbyterian Church (USA) will cease to exist within the lifetimes of those in our senior high school youth groups.[2] We can promise to seek the peace, unity and purity of the church. We can form task forces and practice tolerance. But, in fact, these vows have had no positive or real effect in producing what they promise.

The Presbyterian Church (USA) is at a time of profound crisis. Arguably, this is greater and more dangerous than any crisis faced in 150 years. Twice the church has split over similar (and yet unresolved?) issues. The church, since the modernist-fundamentalist controversies of the 1930s, has been reluctant to seriously address issues of theology in the naïve hope – both tacit and explicit – that this will promote peace and unity. But this has failed. In spite of all efforts to maintain a semblance of peace or unity, a chasm has continued to spread between conflicting theological positions. The growing rift has now reached a point at which it is impossible to ignore it or leave it unaddressed. There is no real peace in the Presbyterian Church (USA). We are connected, but have no real unity. That we have a single constitution, that all church property is held in trust by the denomination,[3] that we share heritage and name, does not change these simple facts. The conflict between differing theological perspectives within the church has led some to believe that we are, in fact, two different denominations (or even religions!) artificially bound by trust deeds, retirement funds and judicatories and that the different perspectives held across the church are "irreconcilable." Whether that is true remains to be seen. But such perspec-

---

2. Simply speaking statistically, at the current rate of decline, the Presbyterian Church (USA) will disappear around 2055-2060.

3. G-8.0201 in the *Book of Order*.

tives reveal beyond doubt or denial that we are, in fact, wrestling with profound issues that must be courageously and faithfully addressed and resolved if we are to be the church in this time.

The situation before us is dire. To live in denial of this fact, or fail to respond to it appropriately, inevitably will bring about the functional – if not literal – end of the Presbyterian Church (USA). Too many for too long have ignored, denied or hidden from this problem and, thus, have failed the church and its Lord by failing to respond. To proclaim "peace, peace ..." when there is no peace, to make vows with no effort to fulfill them,[4] to ignore the crisis or, worse, not care, in the end are faithless and inappropriate responses. We stand on the edge of a cataclysm that threatens the future of the Presbyterian Church (USA) and every one of its constituent congregations and their members and pastors. The issues involved and the cost of failure are profound. It is essential, therefore, and even required, that all who know and love the Gospel of Jesus Christ study, grasp and appropriately respond to the issues at hand.

---

4. One thinks here not only of the vow to maintain the peace, unity and purity of the church, but also the vow to be a faithful participant within the structures of the church.

Chapter Two

DIRECTION AND AIM
OF THIS PAPER

The purpose and aim of this paper is lead the church in theological reflection in the hope of furthering its peace, unity and purity. It is our goal to present a cogent perspective of the issues involved so that pastors, elders and members of the church may understand both the importance of response and the way to respond.

This is not primarily a study, critique or commentary on the report of the Theological Task Force on Peace, Unity and Purity. While some specific study of the report and its recommendations will be offered, the principle issue of this paper is to address the theological issues that led the General Assembly to create the task force. It is our concern that the underlying issues may be ignored, minimized or lost; and it is our belief that this would eviscerate any hope of procuring and advancing the peace, unity and purity of the church. Consequently, these issues will be raised and compared with the report of the task force.

This is a theological paper. The issues facing the church are deep and require serious study and reflection. "Sound bites" and pop-theology are inadequate for the task and it is now required of the church, at every level, to wrestle with very real and very deep issues. To discuss Christology, hermeneutical theory, ecclesiology, authority and power is not to enter into academic speculation or non-pragmatic idealism. The church primarily is what her beliefs and doctrines make her to be. The practical life, the ministry life and the witness of the church are defined more by her ideals, faith and principles than anything else. And, thus, if her life and witness are to be true and faithful, so must the doctrines and faith that undergird them. The church will never live, much less thrive, when her faith and witness is shaped by each person doing what is right in his or her own eyes.[1] Our peace, unity and purity emerge from the truth and reality of our God, His work in the world, and our faithful understanding, participation and commitment to these realities.

This is not easy work. It requires intellectual wrestling, courage to address difficult and controversial ideas, and genuine spiritual wisdom and discernment. Regretfully, the Presbyterian Church (USA) long has been nervous and apprehensive of genuine theological labor. Instead, we have become content with theological phrases that are ancient, faithful and deep, but unexplained, interpreted or proclaimed. Too often, we affirm such axioms as the "Lordship of Jesus Christ" or the "authority of Scripture" without ever defining what we mean by such terms. Such simple – but deep! – statements beg for and demand explanation, definition and clarification. What do we mean by "lordship?" Who (and what!) is this person Jesus? How are we to appropriately respond and what constitutes an inappropriate response? What does authority mean when we speak of the Bible? What interpretive methods reflect and honor its authority and which deny or annul it? It is obvious that people may interpret Scripture in a variety of ways, but which are right, true and faithful and which fail at these and other levels?

True theological work is hard work that courageously addresses such areas, providing thoughtful, rational and faithful explanations for the good of the church. To say, "Jesus is Lord," is a true and faithful proclamation, but it cannot be called theological work. The church of today needs more than simple statements, however true they may be. The situation before us calls for serious theological work that boldly leads the church into a greater and ever more faithful understanding of God's nature, will and work – and our response to that nature, will and work.

It remains to be seen whether the church will rise to this need. For decades, the Presbyterian Church (USA) has shown little interest in theology. Pragmatism, social justice issues, polity, and pastoral concerns repeatedly have trumped theology and pushed it to the margins in the life of the church. Consequently, each of these areas finds itself ever more isolated from the theological perspective that alone can define its course, purpose and message. Real theological reflection and labor is a lost science (and art) in our church. Worse yet, the church seems unaware that this is so. Content with buzz words, theological axioms and bold claims of faithfulness to the Reformed tradition have deluded

---

1.   Judges 21:25.

many people into believing that our theological work has been done and done well. But apart from a few statements, usually from the denomination's Office of Theology and Worship, the church has shown little interest or skill in theological labor.

This paper is an attempt to reverse this trend, and it is offered in the deep hope that the larger Church understands the need of theological reflection and interpretation and will benefit from it. The emphasis and work is unashamedly theological. With and through it all is in open invitation for the church, at every level, to reflect upon the nature, reality, work, and will of God and to understand what it is to know, worship and proclaim his goodness and reign.

Covering many areas, this paper will begin with some simple definitions. It first will seek to explain the terms *evangelical* and *progressive*, as these will be used throughout the whole of the paper. From here, the paper will look at the nature of church conflict through a brief study of Acts 15. Here, we learn of the nature of conflicts within the church, why and how these exist, and how the church is to properly respond to them.

The paper then will jump forward roughly 2,000 years, looking at the nature of the conflict within our church in our time. The nature and character of these differences are profound, but not necessarily obvious. If we are to know and enjoy peace, unity and purity, we must truly, fairly and accurately understand the nature and issues creating strife and division. Having looked briefly at conflict, both ancient and modern, the paper also will look briefly at the vast issue of ecclesiology.

The paper then will move from the more abstract to the specific, from the ideal of the church to the final report of the task force. This will begin with an assessment of its theological work. There are many positive and hopeful points in the report, but there also is much that remains unsaid and, thus, in doubt. From these, we will look specifically at the report's fifth recommendation.

The paper will conclude with a call to minimalist subscriptionism, under the belief that we no longer may function without a basic agreement on what constitutes the essentials of faith and practice within the church.

Chapter Three

TERMS: EVANGELICALS AND PROGRESSIVES

L abels are always risky. They may carry with them historical or interpretive "baggage" that forces them to express more than may be intended. They may be, or felt to be, pejorative and, thus, unfair or intentionally inaccurate. Some are so broadly used in so many contexts that they bear no precise meaning or clear definition. Certainly, such labels as "conservative" and "liberal" or "left" and "right" may be so criticized and, thus, wisely avoided. Certainly, these terms and others, like "centrist" or "moderate," are wholly relative and, thus, without any inherent meaning when separated from their correlation to either or both poles.

Nevertheless, in spite of the difficulties and dangers, it usually is helpful and often required that some label be used to define the issues, perspectives and persons involved. Believing this to be so, and with full awareness that the terms are neither perfect nor without "baggage," we will use the terms *evangelical* and *progressives* (and their respective cognates) to reflect the two sides within the debates and struggles addressed in this paper. The reasons for this are obvious, if imperfect. First, the words accurately reflect and convey the realities, ideas and methodologies involved. Second, each is used regularly by both sides as appropriate self-descriptions.[1] And, finally, the historical context – both

---

1. For example, the Witherspoon Society frequently has stated on its Web site that it offers news "from a progressive perspective." The magazine *The Progressive* long has been a voice of social justice issues that, while generally secular, reflects nearly identical values and perspectives. An article titled "Taking on the Religious Right" (Z Activism Online, http://zmagsite.zmag.org/JulAug2005/chenelle-0705.html) describes progressivism as the antitheses of the "religious right." Interestingly, the use of the term "progressive" to describe a theological perspective or methodology is older than many may know. It was used as both a self-description and critical assessment of New School theology in the Presbyterian Church through the 19th century.

ancient and postmodern – allow these terms to more deeply express the depth, reason and nature of the conflict we face.

But if labels are to be used, it is crucial that they be accurately and fairly defined. Huge issues are facing the Presbyterian Church (USA) and have critically damaged the peace, unity and purity we seek. The terms "evangelical" and "progressive," because of their historical use and accurate reflection of the ideas at stake, can be quite useful in describing and addressing the theological and methodological issues involved. But it remains that both, briefly and accurately, be defined so that the dialogue offered in and beyond this paper might proceed with an appropriate understanding.

A definition of progressive theology is, in many ways, an oxymoron.[2] Progressivism is wary of definitions that are fixed, timeless and objective, preferring instead a dynamic, contemporary and subjective understanding of itself, its message and its work. Any definition of progressivism or progressive theology that statically limits or denies its intrinsic plurality likely will be viewed by its adherents as shallow and inaccurate. That is to say, progressive theology inherently is pluralistic and broad and, thus, by definition, difficult to define. Nevertheless, certain statements may be made. First, its adherents endeavor to create a theology that is both Reformed and ecumenical. The traditions of Calvin and other reformers are valued, honored and received "with critical respect."[3] But progressives want to clearly acknowledge that there is more than one way of being Reformed, and certainly more ways of being Christian than Reformed.

Progressivism, while seeking to honor the Reformed tradition, would be seen as part of a larger Christian and even religious culture. Believing that God has spoken through more than just the Reformed branch of the Christian faith and, for that matter, through other religions and experiences, allows progressives to see revelation across a broad plane. The person of Jesus accurately and powerfully reveals the grace of God and, thus, is of extreme importance. But the grace of God revealed in Jesus is so powerful that it cannot be isolated or singularly bound to Jesus. Rather, the grace of God manifests across the whole of creation. Thus,

---

2.   For a fuller description of progressive theology from a self-described progressive theologian, see the helpful statement at http://www.witherspoonsociety.org/ottati_address.htm. This is the text of an address, titled "Some Characteristics of Progressive Presbyterian Theologies," that Douglas F. Ottati made at the Witherspoon Society luncheon June 16, 2002, in Columbus, Ohio, during the 214th meeting of the General Assembly of the Presbyterian Church (USA).

3.   Ibid.

progressives reject simple distinctions between the sacred and profane, the Christian faith and faith in general, special revelation and general revelation. The pluralistic character of progressivism leads its adherents to see and hear God through a broad range of voices, acts and places. Not only is revelation broad, it is progressive – unfolding and enlarging through grand events and personal experience. Yet, all of these, because of the very breadth and progress of revelation, only continue to unveil God's transforming grace. Progressives hold that salvation comes through grace alone. But this grace is so extravagant and generous that it cannot be limited to one simple perspective or experience, but may be expected to manifest itself in and through other religions and faiths. This makes progressivism extremely hopeful and optimistic.

Thus, progressives would prefer to describe themselves as theocentric rather than Christocentric. That is not to say – again – that Jesus is unimportant or irrelevant. Rather, Jesus is vitally important, not as the object or the center of faith, but an important point of its revelation. Jesus reveals God's grace and love, but the focus and interest of faith is not so much Jesus but the God who is behind him and working in and through him. Nor is Jesus made the center or object of revelation. Jesus "demonstrates and discloses that God is faithful"[4] and, thus, shapes our picture of God. Christ, then, serves as a window – perhaps even the largest and clearest window – into the gracious heart of God. But he is not the only window, nor is the window meant to be the object of our faith and witness. Jesus unveils or reveals the grace of God. We are saved by this grace alone, but not Christ alone.

Progressivism also is profoundly pragmatic. Its interest or goal is found more in the dynamic of a changed world than in a changed life. That is not to say that privatized or inner spiritual experiences are of no value or to be disdained. But progressivism cares more for addressing issues of injustice, inequality, ecology, poverty, gender, and other social ills and problems. Progressivism, in its pragmatism, is profoundly humane, ever seeking for the full inclusion and restoration of the outcast and disenfranchised. This, coupled to the broad view of both grace and revelation, leads progressives to openly accept a wide diversity of beliefs and lifestyles. Grace, revelation and pragmatic actions that right any perceived wrongs all combine to define the positions, faith, expectations, and practices of progressives. This cannot be overstated. In progressive theology, the concepts of grace, revelation and practical

---

4. Ibid.

response intertwine. Because of the efficacy and breadth of grace, its revelation may be found in a variety of places, voices and experiences. Because God reveals himself through many and diverse means, few (none?) should be excluded as incapable of receiving, knowing or bearing his revelation of grace. And anything that breaks the power of injustice, regardless of the source or larger message, may be seen as part of God's redeeming love and grace.

While progressivism is difficult to describe because of its dynamic and pluralistic nature, an accurate definition of evangelicalism is equally difficult, but for very different reasons. Evangelicalism, while being less fluid, is far older and more widely used. Across the centuries, many definitions – some accurate, some not; some friendly and some pejorative – have combined to create a word so broad in meaning as to be almost meaningless. But it is this history and the fact that its roots lie in the Bible itself that renders this word important and illumining.

Evangelical comes from the Greek word *euangelion*[5] meaning, literally, good news and referring to the message of salvation made available through the atoning sacrifice of Jesus Christ. This simple summary touches upon many important characteristics. First, evangelicalism and the evangelical message essentially is optimistic, hopeful and positive. It is good news. It refers to the will and work of the Triune God, who is for us, and to the message of how this has occurred. Even where this message is hard or perceived as judgmental, the aim and goal only and always is positive as the lost are found, the broken made whole, and the sinful redeemed. This optimistic and hopeful message is further enhanced by the focus upon the fact that this salvation is wholly the work of the grace of God, who has made our plight and need his own. The evangelical message is centered on the joyous good news that God was in Christ reconciling the world to himself, and this work is efficacious and gracious.

Evangelicalism is missional. It is the message of God's act of bringing salvation and the means by which it may be known and experienced. Even more, it sees this proclamation as the means by which this salvation comes to people and is received by them. The message of the Gospel is seen as unique and authoritative and, thus, entails an appeal to repentance, decision and conversion from that which is false to that

---

5. The word *euangelion* occurs in 73 verses in the NA27 Greek text. The definitive reference work, *The Theological Dictionary of the New Testament*, uses 30 pages to describe the fullness of meaning and the importance of the word and its cognates.

which God demands and offers. Not only is grace uniquely bound to the person and work of Jesus, the message of the church – if it is to be truly a message of grace – is singularly bound to his incarnation, life, teaching, death, resurrection, and ascension.

Even more precisely, the Gospel message is focused upon the cross and the atoning work of Christ. The evangelical message, from the preaching of Paul to the preaching of Billy Graham, has had no interest in human religion, spirituality or rituals. Its interest always and only has been upon the utterly unique and incomparable sacrifice occurring with the death of Christ. Thus, Paul could write:

> For Christ did not send me to baptize but to preach the gospel, and not with words of eloquent wisdom, lest the cross of Christ be emptied of its power. For the word of the cross is folly to those who are perishing, but to us who are being saved it is the power of God. For it is written, "I will destroy the wisdom of the wise, and the discernment of the discerning I will thwart." Where is the one who is wise? Where is the scribe? Where is the debater of this age? Has not God made foolish the wisdom of the world? For since, in the wisdom of God, the world did not know God through wisdom, it pleased God through the folly of what we preach to save those who believe. For Jews demand signs and Greeks seek wisdom, but we preach Christ crucified, a stumbling block to Jews and folly to Gentiles, but to those who are called, both Jews and Greeks, Christ the power of God and the wisdom of God.[6]

These words reflect the perspective and message that has characterized the evangelical perspective across 2,000 years. This belief – that the Father has demonstrated his grace and love through the death of his Son in our place – has rendered all other philosophies, theologies, religions, and rituals shallow, uninteresting and powerless.

Consequently, grace is bound to and explained in and through this event. Grace is not an esoteric kindness or abstract acceptance, but the primary characteristic of a specific act within time and space. Grace is not a divine benevolence generally offered, but a divine act precisely offered as the means of reconciliation. Grace is a description of this event and its effect. Grace describes not a general attitude, but the mysterious exchange wherein our sins become no longer ours, but Christ's; and Christ's righteousness remains no longer his alone, but ours.

---

6. 1 Corinthians 1:17-24. Paul summarizes his message by stating: "And I, when I came to you, brothers, did not come proclaiming to you the testimony of God with lofty speech or wisdom. For I decided to know nothing among you except Jesus Christ and him crucified" (1 Corinthians 2:1-2).

On the cross, God addressed sin, showing its depth and severity, exercising his righteous judgment of sin by evoking the penalty of death, yet bearing this penalty himself so that we might, in and because of this, be ransomed, healed, restored, and forgiven. Jesus Christ "has not only borne man's enmity against God's grace, revealing it in all its depth, he has borne the far greater burden, the righteous wrath of God against those who are enemies of His grace, the wrath which must fall on us."[7] Thus, grace, within the evangelical tradition, means the gift of salvation freely given in and through the cross where Christ gave his life as an atoning sacrifice.[8] To define grace apart from this event is to understand nothing of either grace or the cross.

The evangelical faith and witness are unashamedly Christocentric. The person and work of Christ, as the primary work of God for our salvation, is held and proclaimed as the one way of salvation. The power of the Christ event – from incarnational birth to ascension – is seen as so uniquely magnificent that all other points of grace pale in comparison. Jesus Christ, of course, is not the only place or point of grace. Indeed, every breath we draw, every beat of our hearts, every act of love received is a gift of God and, thus, an act of grace. But these, for all their value, wonder and good, are but pale impressions of God's defining act of grace seen in the person and work of Jesus. The evangelical, therefore, does not deny grace broadly given and experienced. But a distinction is made between this general grace and special grace, between gifts commonly given and the gift uniquely given in Christ, between gifts in life and the gift of life that leads to salvation. For evangelicals, grace never is allowed to describe and abstract benevolence, nor is it isolated from the concrete event of the incarnation. Here alone is grace defined, understood and received.

Evangelicals are people of Christ because they are people of the Word. Scripture is not merely important. Human authors in specific historical settings and contexts were divinely inspired to produce the authoritative record of God's revelation. The Bible is not God, nor does it replace him or stand in his stead; rather, it serves as the witness to God-saving works in history. And because the focus of these saving acts in Scripture is Jesus Christ, evangelicals have centered their faith, witness

---

7.   Barth, Karl; *Church Dogmatics*; (T&T Clark Publishers; Edinburgh; 1969); Vol. II.1; p. 152.

8.   "He is the atoning sacrifice for our sins, and not only for ours but also for the sins of the whole world" (1 John 2:2). Love, like grace, is not understood in abstract terms, but as the act of Christ's sacrifice on the cross.

and life upon him. This reflects the simple and profoundly important fact that evangelicals passionately strive to remain faithful to Scripture.

There remains one final point that must be addressed before moving on from describing the distinctions and beliefs of progressives and evangelicals. The above definitions are relatively idealized and bear, perhaps, an antipodean character. The realities, of course, are a bit more complex. Neither may be properly understood as simple opposites or even being mutually exclusive. Nor do they reflect the whole of the Christian theological spectrum. Some may read these descriptions and feel that neither adequately or fully describes their perspective or beliefs. Some may leave this section feeling they are, in reality, an "evangelical progressive" or a "progressive evangelical." Some may wish for other titles or descriptions – more left, more right, or more centrist. Some may wish to be forever free of all such attempts at definition.

None of this, of course, ultimately matters. In the end, regardless of label or self-description, the only thing of value is whether or not what we say and believe is true and our methods of discovering this are valid. The title does not matter nearly as much as the reality it attempts to know and describe. Is what we believe real? Is it true and valid? How has this been determined? Is our search for truth and our description of truth appropriate to the object discovered and described?

At issue is not merely who we are within the Christian spectrum or how we describe ourselves. Something far deeper and more significant is at risk. In the end, it is not about us, or what we think or believe, or what we call ourselves. In the Christian faith, and especially within its Reformed branch, the focus has been – and must always remain – upon God. The Gospel is his story. It is about the Father's heart, the Son's sacrifice, and the Spirit's sanctifying work which, together, bring redemption to a fallen and hurting human race. The task of theology is to determine the means by which this reality may be known and accurately described. At issue is nothing less than the truth of God and the truth of who we are. And to fail, in methodology or conclusions, is to live a lie and proclaim a lie.

Labels may be helpful, or they may be problematic. In the end, however, the label matters little. The future and life of the Presbyterian Church (USA) will not depend upon self-descriptions, definitions, or perspectives defined and chosen. It depends upon us accurately and rightly knowing the truth about God and the truth about ourselves. It depends upon us having the right approach, right attitude and right methods. And, ultimately, it depends upon us accurately, rightly and truly knowing God. Anything less, regardless of its label or claim, is only an impotent and vapid counterfeit.

Chapter Four

THE CHURCH IN CONFLICT[1]
CONFLICT IN THE APOSTOLIC CHURCH – ACTS 15

Conflict is not new to the church, but has moved through and around it since its birth. Theological and ecclesial conflicts frequently are described and addressed in the pages of Scripture. Thus, we move here to Acts 15 and a look at the church's handling of a faith-threatening controversy. It is our purpose to use this example of church conflict within ancient times to better understand and address the conflicts we face today in the Presbyterian Church (USA).

We learn from the beginning that the question facing the first century church was one of ultimate importance as it dealt with and explained the nature and means of salvation.[2] While centering around the proper understanding of the law and the rite of circumcision, the theological issues and subsequent conflict were about something vastly greater and more significant. Swirling around and through questions of the law's place and use were the more pressing and important questions of how one is saved, what is required and how, in the end, one may stand righteous and accepted before God. This produced a "sharp dispute"[3] between those who held that adherence to the law in some way was required of the Christian, and Paul and Barnabas and their message and

---

1. This section is heavily shaped and influenced by Karl Barth's *Conflict in the Church* published in *Leben und Glauben*, July 10, 1937, as an attempt to interpret and address the conflicts tearing apart the German church under the shadow of Adolf Hitler. Obviously, the situation of that day and ours is profoundly different. But the theological issues are remarkably similar and provide insight into the nature of church conflict, broadly experienced, and the way it is to be understood and addressed.

2. Acts 15:1.

3. Acts 15:2.

theology of the exclusive, perfect and final sufficiency of Christ.

What brings about such sharp disputes within the church? We are told here that strife arises when, from within the church, there emerge people of good intention and sincere hope who, nevertheless, have lost a proper understanding of the grace of the Lord Jesus Christ.[4] While not explicitly or completely renouncing this grace and its unique redeeming and reconciling power, they have placed alongside and in addition to it – as if anything could stand beside it! – obedience to the law as a condition and requirement of salvation.[5] This simple addition to the message of grace; this subtle and, at first glance, innocuous change; in fact ran utterly contrary to the message of the church since Pentecost – thus, threatening its very existence, proclamation and future. The consequences and weight of this change cannot be overstated as it mocks God[6] and, through its disrupting the peace and unity of the church, damages the souls of those for whom Christ died.[7]

The loss of peace, unity and purity are inevitable wherever and whenever the church misunderstands, rejects, annuls, or redefines the grace of God made ours in Christ. Within the Catholic, Protestant and Reformed traditions, grace is the defining characteristic of both God's act on our behalf and the character of our relationship with him. Grace is the singularly precise description of God's work of redemption and our response of repentance and faith. Grace is a concrete reality flowing from the nature of God and manifesting itself precisely and efficaciously in the person and work of the Son. Grace, having its source in the being and will of the Father and manifesting itself in the Son, becomes, by the act of the Spirit, a transformative reality by which our relationship with God is restored and our lives redeemed.

Grace, as understood in Scripture and the Reformed tradition, is not an abstract principle. It is not an ambivalent acceptance of any and all. It is not a benign tolerance. Grace is a precise act of the Triune God concretely manifesting itself and affecting change through each person of the Godhead. Grace, as understood in the Scriptures, always bears a dialectical character as it necessarily includes and reveals both God's beneficence and judgment. Grace is more than mere kindness. It simultaneously expresses the fact of our sin and rebellion and, thus, estrange-

---

4.   Acts 15:11.

5.   Acts 15:1, 5, 24.

6.   Acts 15:10.

7.   Acts 15:24.

ment from God and the gift of his mercy, whereby it neither is overlooked nor punished, but dealt with in a way that honors God's holiness and love, wrath and mercy.

Acts 15 is an account of the church in danger of losing this understanding of God's grace. That is not to say, of course, that Paul's opponents flagrantly and explicitly denied the reality or concept of grace. What they denied was Paul's view of grace and his insistence that it is utterly and solely able and necessary for salvation. On this, his opponents disagreed – holding that, while it was important, good and even real, it was alone insufficient and in need of something further. Again, it was not that one side believed in grace and the other did not; rather, the conflict revolved around very different understandings of the nature, efficacy and uniqueness of grace. Acts 15 is about a division and conflict that occurred as different factions fought to determine which understanding of grace most accurately and faithfully expressed God's will and work in Christ. And with this conflict, there was raised within the church the question of what exactly is the Gospel, what is the message of the church and how is it properly to describe the human condition, God's act of redemption, and the effect this act produces. When grace is misunderstood, the truth of the Gospel is at risk.

Grace is misunderstood, rejected or annulled in essentially four different (but usually interrelated) ways. The first and most common occurs when the concept of grace as pure gift is lost and grace, instead, becomes a reward for proper spirituality, piety or morality. Gift becomes reward and salvation a payment earned. Second – and no less common or influential – is the rendering of grace null by considering it insufficient or inadequate and, thus, in need of being fortified through additional means. Here, one receives the gift of grace but adds to it – through obedience, works, piety, etc. – whatever may be lacking. Third is the concept or teaching that holds that grace, while helpful, is not needed at all. This may mean in its entirety (one thinks here of Pelagianism) or only in part (semi-Pelagianism) but, in either case, the grace of God, in part or completely, is unnecessary. And, fourth, grace is misunderstood and lost when special grace is confused with general grace and understood as part of the natural order, or human nature. Here, one does not need special or saving grace because their natural condition has sufficiently made them "right" in the eyes of God. Each reflects a different facet of what is a single problem: The necessary and central character of grace is lost, rejected or annulled through each and all of these.

What, then, happens when grace is lost? A struggle must develop. It cannot be stopped; indeed, it must not. Paul and Barnabas, by their unwavering faith in the unique efficacy of the grace of Christ, would not yield an inch to their opponents,[8] even for the sake of peace and unity. Where the truth of the Gospel message is attacked or lost, God also is attacked and lost, and peace and unity dissolved. Thus, they could not turn from the struggle because there is no higher truth or good than the free gift of grace given through the person and work of Christ. To lose this would mean the death of the church.

But if struggle cannot, must not, be avoided, it also is essential that it be addressed rightly. Conflict must not be denied, either explicitly or implicitly, in the hope of maintaining peace. Where the essence of the Gospel is lost or denied, it is incumbent upon the church to bring the issue and conflict before an arbiter or judge who rightly may decide between the two. But how is this done? Acts 15 teaches that the church of Antioch brought the issue to the apostles in Jerusalem, and these apostles arbitrated between the conflicted church.[9] The primary voices were those of Peter[10] and James[11] who, in their speaking, brought in the judgment and authority of the prophets.[12] In the church, in all its crises and conflicts, there always is a judge. We must not think that no higher judge or authority exists above stubborn antagonists and passionate contenders. There is no reason, in the church at least, for believing that everyone may be right or, conversely, no one and, thus, it is in the best interest of peace and unity to merely break off the conflict and agree to disagree. Within the church, there is a judge – a judge who alone can, may and will arbitrate. And that judge is no different today than in Acts or any period of church history: the word of the apostles and the prophets. These are called the foundation of the church,[13] and their practical function is to bind the church to Christ the cornerstone. Then as now, now as then, it is incumbent upon the church to listen to the word of the apostles and the prophets, and to hear from them afresh the truth of God's will and work of grace.

The word of the apostles resulted in a letter sent to Antioch[14] that stated their instructions and will. The word of the apostles and the

---

8.   Galatians 2:5.

9.   Acts 15:2, 6, 22-23.

10. Acts 15:7-11.

11. Acts 15:13-21.

12. Acts 15:15-17.

13. Ephesians 2:20.

14. Acts 15:23-29.

prophets and, thus, the Word of God himself, affirmed that the free grace available in and through Christ is alone the hope and source of God's blessing. The rightness, truth and authority of this Word reduce all in the church of Antioch to silence. And, by this judgment, the message, peace and unity of the church is maintained and advanced. Where the free grace of God in Christ is proclaimed and enjoyed, there the church is fully alive and there God himself is most at work in and through his Word, miracles, conversions, signs and wonders.[15]

In closing, however, it is important to note one final fact. Was this merely an incident of one side (Paul and Barnabas) being "declared right" and the other side being "declared wrong?" If, in fact, this was the case, it is unlikely that either peace or unity would have resulted. In a sense – and this is supremely important – the story is not one of either side being declared right (or wrong) so much as the Word of God being declared true, authoritative, valid, and efficacious. In a sense, none of those involved was placed wholly in the right, even those who rightly proclaimed the word of grace. In the proclamation of the word of the apostles and the prophets, in the defense and articulation of grace, all sides and all involved are declared to be in need of the grace of God in Christ. The Word of God confronts all with the dialectical "no" and "yes" of the Gospel and the fact that "no flesh may glory in his presence."[16] But when the Word of God is spoken and heard, when submission to this Word occurs and a turn from every claim of self-righteousness – be it through works or nature – manifests itself, then there remains no room for offense or accusation. Peace, unity and purity are tightly intertwined, and rise or fall upon our understanding and submission to the grace of God in Christ. Where this Word is heard and received in humble, grateful awe, the church will discover the riches of peace, unity and purity as a gift of grace through the "yes" and "no" of the cross.

---

15. Acts 15:3-4, 12.

16. I Corinthians 1:29.

Chapter Five

CONFLICT IN OUR TIME: THE PRESBYTERIAN CHURCH (USA)

DIFFERENCES BETWEEN EVANGELICALS AND PROGRESSIVES

The differences between evangelicalism and progressivism are profound. This, however, does not necessarily mean obvious. In fact, the shared language, combined with a broad desire to avoid conflict, has encouraged many people to assume that the differences essentially are insignificant. This is a very important point and one worth considering. If the two are saying essentially the same thing; if, in fact, these are merely different ways of explaining the same truth and reality; then the conflict and disunity that has consumed us is both misplaced and easily corrected. Acceptance, tolerance and grace are all that is required and there is nothing left but to "celebrate our diversity."

But if, in fact, there are differences between the two, then the means of achieving peace, unity and purity are far more difficult and the stakes far greater. If the two are more than different names for nearly identical perspectives; if they present different methodologies for discerning truth and different conclusions regarding truth; then something vast and important is at stake. If, in the end, we are about the truth of God and the truth of ourselves, then we courageously must ask if both really are equally valid. And where either or both fail to discover, discern, or respond to truth, this must be recognized, confronted and corrected.

In fact, the differences between the two are not only vast, but arguably mutually exclusive and, thus, at many points irreconcilable. In spite of shared vocabulary, history and structure, evangelicals and progressives are describing two different realities, two different worldviews, two different methodologies, and two different theological perspectives. Evangelical faith shares with progressivism a theocentric

93

emphasis, yet with essential distinctions. Evangelicalism is ever, only and always Trinitarian in its understanding of God. This places its accompanying Christocentrism in perspective. Evangelicalism is not Christomonist – a singular focus upon the person of Christ that ignores or denies the Father and Spirit – but Christocentric. That is, Christ is seen as the center of three crucial issues: revelation, redemption and relationship. Evangelicals hold that while revelation generally occurs, this revelation remains obtuse and incapable of providing salvation. One cannot know God apart from or outside of the person of Jesus, for it is here that God has chosen to reveal his nature and work of redemption. Evangelicalism generally doubts (denies?) that revelation occurs in the breadth or variety held by the progressive school. In light of this, evangelicalism generally holds to the exclusivity of Jesus as the only way to salvation.[1] Jesus is not only the focal point of revelation, he is, through the saving efficacy of this revelation, the single means of salvation. Salvation is something that occurs in and through him. This differs from the perspective held in progressivism, where salvation generally is something that occurs within a person, community or social structure.

While both progressivism and evangelicalism are optimistic, they are for different reasons. The former finds its ground for optimism in the breadth of God's grace, which flows broadly and generously through many conduits. The latter's optimism is founded upon the power and depth of that grace manifesting itself in the singular point of Jesus Christ. The difference is profound and has far-reaching implications. Progressives focus upon the concept of grace, while evangelicals focus on the person in whom it most powerfully manifests itself.

Evangelical faith is a confessional faith, while progressivism is not. That is to say, evangelicalism holds to standards of faith and practice that have been passed down through the centuries. Evangelicalism, though ever striving to deepen and expand its understanding of revelation, seeks it in a way that remains faithful to earlier traditions and the conclusions of the church. The reasons for this are consistent with the larger perspectives of evangelicalism. Because of its Christocentrism and belief that Christ is the focal point of God's revelation, it seeks to affirm and hold to faithful interpretations of this event as they have appeared across time. Progressivism, on the other hand, is only loosely or mildly confessional. Because revelation is progressive and, thus, not bound to the Christ event, past interpretations or expressions of this

---

1. For a helpful study, see James R. Edwards; *Is Jesus the Only Savior?* (Grand Rapids, Mich.; Eerdmans Publishing; 2005).

event are only of limited interest. They may or may not describe how
and where God is revealing himself today.

These again reflect profound differences that affect our understanding and pursuit of peace, unity and purity. At issue, once again, is the
truth about God, how he is known, how he acts, and what he does. Evangelicalism, with its confessional perspective, holds that God has acted
finally and perfectly in Christ, and the purpose of theology is to
describe this event and its implications in faithful detail. Progressivism,
on the other hand, holds that this event, while important, is not unique
and, thus, looks for God's revelation in the grand panoply of human
diversity.

Conflict is not new to the Church. We all may wish this were not so,
but the fact remains that the Church, through the whole of its history,
has had to weather squabbles, strife and schism. Some of these conflicts
center upon issues that are small and isolated in time, place and people.
Examples may include the Bangorian controversy, Bourignioism, *Les
Trembleurs des Cevennes* and countless others that, no doubt, were
pressing to their respective antagonists, but of limited impact and influence upon the larger Church since these did not deal with ultimate
issues at the center of faith, but with marginal questions. Other controversies are universal, threatening the very life of the Church and the
message of the Gospel. One thinks here of Arianism, which championed
a heretical Christology, and Pelagianism, which taught that salvation
was earned and grace helpful, but unnecessary. These ancient conflicts,
unlike the others, were not lost to history, but remain influential to this
very day. It is incumbent upon the Presbyterian Church (USA) to carefully discern the issues at hand and respond appropriately. The church
must be guided by the ancient axiom *in necessaries unitas, in dubiis lib-
ertas, in omnibus caritas* (In necessary things unity, in doubtful things
liberty, in all things charity). Secondary issues, those things we might
call *dubiis* – such as worship styles, music, liturgy, method of baptism,
etc. – allow for and call for a great breadth of liberty. The worship of
God from a pure heart, in Spirit and in truth, is an essential and necessary element of the Christian life. How this worship occurs – high
church or low, seeker sensitive or traditional, organ or guitar – are secondary and non-essential issues. And there, rightly, is a great deal of
freedom to be granted across and within the church as it worships
through a variety of ways.

But there are, and always have been, issues that are neither peripheral
nor secondary, but are necessary, essential and required. The church
never has existed without such essential tenets and practices – even

when not explicitly stated – and often has had to risk her very life to maintain and proclaim them. The uniqueness of Christ's atonement, his duel nature, salvation by grace through faith, his bodily resurrection, and the authority of Scripture are – and always have been – understood and held as essential tenets of the Christian faith. Perhaps more important is the fact these are not doctrines unique to the Reformed tradition, but are held across the whole of the Church for essentially the whole of its existence. Such doctrines are not secondary, but necessary, elements to the church faith, life and witness, and their loss means – at the very least – a complete redefinition of the church and – at worst – its dissolution and loss. While liberty and breadth is to be granted to secondary issues of faith and practice, those doctrines that are necessary to the faith require genuine unity. And, where unity over essential tenets is denied, there can be no hope of peace or purity.

The crisis we face revolves around primary and necessary, not secondary, doctrines. The issues disrupting the peace, unity and purity of the Presbyterian Church (USA) are neither peripheral nor incidental, but are, on the contrary, threatening the life, future and faith of the church. While many of the battles and controversies have swirled around various issues of homosexuality, it would be a grave mistake – indicative of only the simplest discernment – to assume that homosexuality is the real battle or point of primary concern. At stake is something far deeper and, therefore, far more important. The crisis before the Presbyterian Church (USA) today is one that challenges our understanding of God's very nature, how it is that we know him, and how we are healed, restored and forgiven. Thus, at issue is nothing less than the first commandment itself.

We are facing a crisis over the nature, means and reality of revelation. And in this crisis, we are being called to decide whether we will remain faithful to the Reformation principles of faith alone, Scripture alone, grace alone, and Christ alone or whether we will, at the same time, allow revelation and salvation to be found in other places, voices and events. With this, we see again that the issues involved are not peripheral, but central to our Reformed tradition and essential to the Gospel. The divisions and discord so prevalent within our church are theologically bound. Their resolution requires the precision and particularity of our theological confession.[2]

---

2. One of the principle failures of the report of the Theological Task Force on Peace, Unity and Purity in the Presbyterian Church (USA) is its attempt to create peace and unity through process rather than theological unity.

If the issues disrupting the peace, unity and purity of the church were about spirituality, then there may well be a rationale for seeking peace by holding that, in all our diversity, we are seeking the same goal. Such uniformity is within the nature and scope of spirituality. But it is not, and cannot be, a characteristic of theology. The reasons are both obvious and fundamental. Spirituality is a human, not divine, descriptor. It expresses a particularly human quest, characteristic, experience, or feeling. Consequently, it is not about God. It does not describe God or his nature, work, will, or goals. As a description of human feeling, quest and experience, it is incapable of deciding or distinguishing between what is true or false, real or imagined, about the person, will and work of God. But it can, and does, describe a relatively common, even universal, characteristic of human nature because it deals with and explains a characteristic of the human race that has a universality that Christian theology does not. Spirituality is not about God, but about us. Spirituality describes our quest and hunger for the divine, the very diverse means this is pursued and experienced, and the differing beliefs, hopes and practices it values in this process. Because of its breadth, there are both positive and negative elements to spirituality. It accurately and appropriately may describe the methods, approach and quest of any religion, from Christian to Wicca, New Age to Islam. That is to say that, from a Christian perspective, some methods, beliefs and goals of spirituality would be deemed illegitimate and even, perhaps, ungodly. Spirituality accurately may describe the human hunger and quest for spiritual truth or even God, but it does not – nor cannot – describe God in any way.

Theology, on the other hand, is not a description of us, but of God. And where we are involved or included in this description, it is only in terms of contingent relationship. Theology, at least Christian and Reformed theology, never seeks to understand or describe human life and nature in isolation from the Triune God. It never is interested in who we are *per se*, but who we are before God – Father, Son and Holy Spirit – and how we are to appropriately respond to his call, redemption and love. The differences in approach, methods and conclusions cannot be overstated and must not be missed. Theology bears an unavoidable particularity. Within its description of the nature and work of God, there is combined both a positive affirmation and a necessary criticism and rejection of that which is counter to it. Theology cannot simultaneously affirm or describe mutually exclusive realities. It cannot hold in juxtaposition inherent contradictions. One cannot simultaneously affirm that both monotheism and polytheism are true and legitimate. One cannot affirm that Jesus is Lord while affirming that other lords may exist and be equally valid. One cannot affirm Jesus as his or her "Savior" while affirming that others may know "another savior" or way to salvation. Such a view may be appropriate in discussions of spirituality, but it is completely foreign to the Reformed tradition and its theological confession.

Spirituality and theology are not different sides of the same coin, but are completely disparate in their assumptions, methods, beliefs, and goals. One does not "look up" and the other "down" and, in their combination, reveal truth; rather, each looks at the totality of life and existence and describes, from its own particular worldview, what is real, true and good. In the end, these are completely different, mutually exclusive, worldviews.

It is essential, if we genuinely are to understand each other, that we clearly define the terms we use and grasp that behind them may lie very different perspectives. Theology requires a precision of language that not always is used or appreciated. This is not only true for theologians wrestling with the deepest issues of our faith; it is required of all who seek to explain their faith and their understanding of God. And it is required of all who would seek the peace, unity and purity of the church, for who can say how these might be attained and what their fulfillment might look like without some common definition.

Shared vocabulary does not mean unity or consensus. Clearly, across the church, there is shared a common vocabulary drawn from the Scriptures and our shared heritage. But it is just as obvious, or should be, that shared words do not mean shared understanding or accepted definition. This fact is broadly evidenced within and without the issues of faith. The word "Christ" may form part of the name of the Disciples of Christ, The Church of Jesus Christ Latter Day Saints (Mormons), and The Church of Jesus Christ Christian (Aryan/white supremacist) but, clearly, the understanding and definition used by each is radically different. In fact, in spite of the same vocabulary, it is accurate to say that each is describing a "Christ" that is utterly different and unrelated to that proclaimed and believed by either of the other two. Such ambiguity is not isolated to areas of faith. The official name of North Korea is the Democratic People's Republic of Korea. But, in spite of the impressive claims of its name, it is neither democratic nor a republic, but one of the world's worst examples of inhumane repression and injustice. Clearly, one may use terms such as "Christ," "republic" and "grace" without any consistency with past or broader definitions, or agreement with others who use the same term.

Progressivism, with its emphasis on grace, may appear to affirm the

Reformation axiom of grace alone. The emphasis placed upon God's grace by progressives may convince many people that the two sides are not far off. This, however, is an inaccurate and destructive assumption. The grace proclaimed from the progressive side is not that bound singularly to the person and work of Christ as our catholic, Protestant and Reformed tradition always has held, but is separated from Christ and held as an abstract principle. Grace in progressivism describes the divine benevolence and a diverse breadth of revelatory acts across time, space and every human dimension. It largely, however, is isolated from Christ and the incarnation – the very point that the Bible repeatedly and consistently describes as the locus, definition and work of grace.

The concept and understanding of grace is central to the debates reverberating across our denomination. The issue tearing at the heart and life of the Presbyterian Church (USA) is not sexuality or ordination standards, but something far more important. Pious acts and orthodox vocabulary veil and obscure this fact and lead many people to believe the struggle is something different than it is. What is at stake – and the reason the struggle is crucial and necessary – is that ultimately it concerns our understanding of God, how we know him and respond to him, and what we are to believe and proclaim. At issue are profoundly disparate views of God, humanity and salvation, and the church is being asked, once again, what is the truth? What reality does grace describe? Which definition of grace best and most accurately describes the truth and reality of God and his work of salvation? Until such theological questions openly and courageously are addressed – and answered – there is little hope of peace, unity or purity in the Presbyterian Church (USA) and we will have to settle for tawdry and powerless alternatives.

In the pursuit of peace, unity and purity, we often find ourselves tempted to allow peace to trump either unity or purity. Indeed, the temptation toward tolerance at all costs is a characteristic of our postmodern age. Tolerance has the tacit appeal of neither demanding nor requiring a decision or, to put it theologically, a confession. In the end, however, tolerance is incapable of bringing real peace or unity, much less purity, to the church. Tolerance is not a cognitive value. It is a social value and a political value and, as such, may shape relationships and even produce a cease-fire – but it cannot discern, describe or promote truth. It can whitewash over the issues and act as though they do not exist, but tolerance has no power to address, correct or reconcile our differences.

For decades, the Presbyterian Church (USA) has sought peace through simply ignoring or denying the depth and breadth of the differences between its members. We hear repeated calls to tolerance, to celebrate our diversity and to connectionalism, while the real differences between us are ignored. But this merely is dressing the wound, this merely declaring "peace, peace…" when there is no peace. Mistakenly effected peace treaties, however, temporarily will hide or deny the real issues and, thus, only increase conflict.

Chapter Six

The Nature and Character of the Church

In the end, most people seek a revival or renewal that consists of little more than a change, correction or restoration of doctrine, practice or principles. Few address genuine spiritual realities, repentance, humility, service, and life-changing worship. Most offers and attempts to bring spiritual health and vibrancy to the church are, in the end, simply prosaic and jejune articulations that deny the church what it needs most. It has mastered religion and history, while losing all awareness and enjoyment of the living God.

We have forgotten Thoreau's admonition in *Walden* to be wary of all who require new clothes without also demanding a new wearer of the clothes. The Christian faith is not about externals, forms and functions; it is about life remade, reborn and realized, and this not in mere words or theory, but in hope-filled, joyous experience. The Christian faith is about the fascinating, good and wonderful God of all creation who, in the persons of Father, Son and Holy Spirit, has addressed our helplessness with tenderness and freely offered us what we never could otherwise know or own. The Christian faith is about the Gospel of Jesus Christ, in whom God was reconciling the world to himself and making from a fallen and helpless race a new body of priests holy, pure and pleasing to him. The outward forms of the church are irrelevant if we have lost sight of this center or fail to ensure that it burns white hot.

To understand, describe or posit the church in any form that ignores or diminishes the dynamic presence of Jesus is to miss the glory, goal and life of the church altogether. The church exists not as an organization, foundation or institution, but as the body of the living Christ. This

distinction is not only important, it is crucial.[1] It is a distinction, however, that often is lost in language and doctrine that reflects something
less, yet are sufficiently valid and true to mislead many people. The
church, though, is the Body of Christ, not the institution of Christ. An
institution exists as the fruit and work of the one who institutes it, a definition that many people might find adequate or accurate of the church.
Ultimately, though, it fails to grasp, enjoy and experience the precious
power and presence of the living Christ in its very midst. The church
does not exist merely to proclaim and perpetuate the 2,000 year-old
teachings of Jesus.

All this raises theological questions of far-reaching impact: What is
the church? What does the Father will for the Body of Christ and how
are we to faithfully and obediently respond? Is he at work among and
through us, even those of us who go by the name Presbyterian? What
may we learn of this work from the Scriptures, our confessions and the
Spirit? To look at the church, to study its struggles, claims, hopes and
call, is, in the end, to wrestle with the deepest and most important theological issues of salvation, reconciliation and the kingdom of God. It is
in the church and through the church that the theories of God's love and
mercy actually are to manifest themselves in tangible realities.

Perhaps the reason people are drifting from the church is that they
see too few manifestations of what the *Book of Order*, *The Book of Confessions* and the Spirit of the living God all proclaim we should have
and know. It is interesting, and perhaps even tragic, that the descriptions
of the church's character and endowment as described in Scripture, the
confessions and theology differ so much from how most of us actually
experience it. The reality described and the reality we actually and regularly experience too often are so disparate as to suggest and produce
frightening conclusions. Some people have proclaimed that the church
described in such glorious and victorious terms is that of the eschaton
and not one to be known or lived in this age. Others turn from spiritual
ideals unmet and unfulfilled to a church more concerned and centered
upon the material, temporal and pragmatic. And it matters not if this
manifests itself in conservative prosperity doctrines or liberal social
agendas – both have sold their birthright of the living presence of Jesus

---

1. Crucial, from the Latin *cruc* or *crux* (cross), points to the essence of a thing. For
    the church, this means that not only what is at issue is essential and necessary, but
    also is to be drawn from and built upon the center of the faith, Jesus Christ and
    him crucified (1 Corinthians 2:2 *et. al.*) The church's health is determined by the
    degree to which it takes up and lives a cruciform existence.

for a pottage of material realities and vapid platitudes. Others simply leave the church and even the faith, drawing from experience that there is no reality or truth to the theories. A church that claims nothing less than being the body and, thus, the material presence of Christ in the world, offers only rules, ritual and religion and will neither attract nor change the world.

There no longer is any question that American culture is post-Christian. Not only are most churches in decline, those people who attend are less certain, less knowledgeable, and less involved with the Gospel than at any time in American history. There is no question or debate that the church is in need of renewal, revival and reform. What remains open – and controversial – is how this is to come, what it is to proclaim, and what we hope it will provide. And it remains open as to if and who will proclaim this message of life and revival, who will be willing to step out – perhaps fearful, yet courageously – to be a people of the Word in this day, to this culture.

I propose that the course we must take is one of both looking back and looking forward, of ancient words bound to an eschatological hope, bold prophetic words drawn from the Scriptures and proclaimed in the power and anointing of the living Spirit of God. I suggest what the church needs is to return to its first, and only, love – the Lord Jesus, who exists not as the founder or initiator of the church, but its present, active and working Lord. We must consciously, repeatedly and consistently turn from religion and rituals to a Christ-centered, Spirit-enabled relationship that depends upon, enjoys and reflects the very real presence of Jesus.

The church is described in the New Testament as Christ's "body," as his "flock," his "bride," as God's "people," and even a building. These are all good, revealing and true. But any description of the church – even those provided by the Scriptures – must be properly understood and proclaimed. A proper and true description of the church never will be limited to or centered upon its own characteristics, nature, call, success or failure, or any other concept or description, no matter how accurate or true. The church never can be described in abstraction, but only in relationship. In a similar way, you cannot know or describe me apart from the people with whom I am in relationship. To describe or know me without mention of or understanding of my precious wife, Linda Lee, or my daughters, my parents and friends, is not only shallow, it is to not know me. No person can be known or accurately described apart from relationships, for we are beings in communion. This is no less true for the church. To describe the church by its size, doctrine, history, or

mission is to miss the meaning of the church, regardless of how accurately any of these may have been expressed. At issue is not "What is
the church?" "What is it like?" or "What does it do?" but, rather, "with
whom is the church related, why and how is this so, and what does it
mean?" Ultimately, the church is not an institution unto itself, but a
community in relationship, with the Triune God and with each other,
and by this alone the church is defined.

The presence of Christ alone is the constitutive element of the community of the people of God. Where Jesus is present, the community is
constituted. And, conversely, where Jesus is not present or not recognized and honored and where even the church is unsure of or unaware
of his presence, the community ceases to exist in spite of the apparent
health of its external forms. The community lives and exists by the presence of Christ alone. The church is the living community of the living
Savior and, as such, exists as the community of the saved who know and
enjoy fellowship with the God and Father of our Lord Jesus, in the
power of the Holy Spirit.

Consequently, the church exists as a manifestation of the age of salvation. This means, and we are getting ever more theological here, that
the church can and must be understood not only relationally, but eschatologically. Or, to be even more precise, the church exists as the existential manifestation of an eschatological ontology and corresponding relationship. The church's confession of Jesus as the Christ is bound to the
fact that he is the bringer and provider of salvation, which is nothing
less than an eschatological reality. Jesus came from heaven and dwelt
among us as heaven's reality, truth and goal. His life and work were a
manifestation, not of the best of humanity or human potential, but of
heaven appearing in time. His healing of the sick, lepers and the blind
was but a foretaste of the reality that will find fulfillment in a heaven
empty and devoid of sickness, disease and infirmity. His forgiveness of
sins and grace is a characteristic of eternity actually and concretely
sprinkled into time. His raising the dead – Lazarus, a widow's son and a
little girl – reflects in miniature and foretaste what will occur at the end
of the age. His authority over the demonic is to us (and them!) a glim-
mer of that incandescent radiance that one day will overwhelm this
world of darkness. The Lord's defeat of sin, death and the devil during
and through his life, death and resurrection are all eschatological realities. They are the manifesting in time, in part but truly, of that which we
will taste in fulfillment at the end of the age when Jesus returns to set
all things right.

All that Jesus was and did is to be understood eschatologically. Jesus is not only returning, the returning one is coming to fulfill the work he initiated with his incarnation and continues through his living presence within and through the community.[2] And he is not only coming, he is present within the church manifesting truly, though in part, the realities of heaven.

The community is an outpost of the Kingdom of God. Like Jesus himself, his body is the manifesting in space and time of a future or eternal reality, and the living out in time and space of those relationships characterized and made necessary and available by this reality. And it is this, not because of some inherent right or character, but only because of the presence of the One who came and will come again. He exists and works amidst the community as the incarnate Son of God and coming King. He is the bringer of the *eschaton's* realities. By his sovereign and gracious will, he calls his sheep by name and creates the community that he leads and protects as shepherd.

Arguably, the vapid, shallow, religious character of the church grew when the community lost interest in and awareness of the present Christ and an understanding of its own eschatological character. No longer the expected One present through the faith and relationship of the community, he instead becomes bound or limited to a vague or ethereal presence, only barely real or not real at all. Like those at a memorial service who might say of the deceased, "He's not really gone as long as we all remember him in our hearts," Jesus' presence is limited to memories, truths or narratives of great days and times. But the church is robbed and stripped of its life whenever it loses sight of its own eschatological nature and replaces the eschatological Christ with one who is "there" merely as principle, memory, concept, or precept, but not in fact. Nevertheless, it is a common error. Jesus' work and presence takes on an all but entirely passive form in sermons, sacraments or the being of the church. Jesus takes on a reality within the church not unlike most of our relationships with the World Bank: We know it is there and doing something, but we are not sure what or how and have no expectation that it will touch, influence, change, or help our immediate existence.

The danger in all this lies in the fact that the presence of Christ, while declared real and true, is practically and essentially irrelevant. It

---

2. This is the meaning of Acts 1:1 "The first account I composed, Theophilus, about all that Jesus began to do and teach...." What Jesus *began* to do, Luke described in his Gospel narrative; what Jesus continued to do, he intends to describe in what follows in Acts. The church lives in the hope that all the wonders, love and grace Jesus did during his lifetime are but the start of what he would continue to do daily in and through the church, and what he will conclude with his return.

has no experiential reality, no volitional reality, and no existential reality, but exists as mere noetic principle. The church fails to experience or demonstrate the saving, redeeming power she claims to hold and know. This is because of, and will lead further into, the loss of her essential eschatological character. Such a church may reflect Christianity or Christendom, but not the living and present Christ. And, in the end, this is fatal. The church must recover its understanding and experience of its eschatological character and reality. It must understand how the essential truth of its eschatological ontology shapes its responsibilities, expectations and the realization of its benefits.

The eschatological church shapes its responsibilities in light of the future, not the present, age. We work to form and display, within the temporal and spatial order, the realities and truth of the eternal kingdom of God. This leads specifically to three responsibilities, the first for those in leadership, the second for those who are led and the third for all members of the salvation community.

Those in leadership have but one major responsibility – to bring those under their care and shepherding into the presence of God. This is the primary task and work of those who lead worship, preach the Gospel and teach any age. Our singular and uniting task is to bring people into the Lord's holy and grace-filled presence. This requires a profound level of humility, spiritual wisdom and maturity. It requires a heart and will soft to the Word and Spirit of God. The proper function of leadership is found not in power or prestige, but in humble guidance to the One who alone is shepherd of our souls. The work of leading the church is nothing if not a spiritual work and the labor of all who lead the community. Every task, from administrating to baptizing to commissioning, is to prepare the way of the Lord, to make rough places smooth and to build for the people a highway to and for our God. And who is adequate for such a task? Our adequacy comes not through seminaries, professional seminars or the call of church and presbytery, but from the depth of our relationship to the living Christ and to the degree that we live our lives in his image. The standard of leadership within the church must be raised to match and model eschatological realities. This means nothing less than approaching pulpits and classrooms, mission fields and fellowship, with the fragrance of heaven hanging over us like cologne. Only here will the ministries of the church be seen for what they truly are: the call and manifestation of God who, even now, is reconciling the world to himself through Christ.

Those who are led need the same qualities and same pursuits. These qualities and attributes are no less important for those being led and shepherded. Indeed, much that occurs in the life of the community, from worship to missions, is determined by the spiritual depth, humility and hunger of the people. It is incumbent upon the community to approach worship, Scripture, prayer, service, and fellowship hungry for God and fully expectant. But in spite of the similarities, there are differences. Where the leader comes with the call and authority to speak for God and lead the body into his will and way, those led must come as expectant listeners ready to respond to the will of God proclaimed in Scripture, sermon and lesson.

One of the most difficult responsibilities required of all who dwell within the eschatological community of the church is submission to authority. Humility comes hard, as it is contrary to the flesh and our sinful natures. Authority and authority structures, however, exist under God's sovereignty and his own authority. The struggle within every life is that of relinquishing authority over our own lives, bending the knee in submission, and obediently following as the Lord desires and wills. Unfortunately, the church too often is characterized by those who are more interested in exercising their rights and authority than in submitting to Christ and those he has called to lead. This is harmful in any organization or body, but it is fatal in the church. Submission to authority structures, to those God has placed over us, is a characteristic of heaven and something required of the church if it is to enjoy and know the fullness of its eschatological nature.

The eschatological church shapes its expectations according to the future, not the present, age. Our participation in the life and work of the community is different from anything the world has to offer. In the genuine community of Christ, the eschatological community, the benefits, blessings and realities find concrete manifestation. Forgiveness may be known, not as psychological principle, but as ultimate reality affecting the whole of one's life. The eschatological community announces, provides and demonstrates within the temporal order the eternal realities of forgiveness and reconciliation. With this comes peace – peace between our fallen and warlike race and our heavenly Father, and peace between one another. And peace, like forgiveness, is not a peace given by or characteristic of this world and all the world gives, but a peace that is given by the Lord Jesus himself that passes beyond description and understanding. Peace is available because we are forgiven and removed from under God's righteous judgment. We have been transferred from the kingdom of this age into the kingdom of Christ and we are to display the unbounded, unfettered and unrestricted joy that comes from being declared and made right in God's eyes.

Forgiveness and peace are but the beginning of God's heavenly gifts. The eschatological church expects and enjoys God's healing presence. While this – and all these manifestations – are to find ultimate fulfill-ment only in heaven in the wake of Christ's return, and while healing does not always follow our prayers, physical and emotional healing may be known in our time. This goes for all of the Spirit's gifts and power – all of which are eternal realities, and all of which may be tasted within our time. God gives to his church the gifts necessary to proclaim the good news in word and power. To each member of the eschatological community, gifts are given to be used for the glory of God, the expan-sion of his kingdom and the building up of the Body of Christ.

The community itself can be expected, in the light of eschatological realities manifesting themselves within it, to take on a wholly new and unique character. Through its 2,000-year history, the church more often has displayed a worldly, not heavenly, nature. The lack of love and serv-ice, the presence of bickering, complaining, greed and countless forms of immorality, too often have rendered the Church of Jesus Christ indis-tinguishable from the world. But we can expect more. As an eschatolog-ical community, we can and must exhibit nothing less than the commu-nity of heaven actively and intentionally living in love and service.

We can expect God's guidance and protection. We rest in the promise that he who began his eschatological work in you will be faithful to complete it until the day of Christ Jesus; that is, the day the *eschaton* manifests itself in ultimate reality. The church moves ahead not by pro-grams, fads, principles or claims, but by and in the very present and effective Spirit of God. We are led into our future and protected as we move forward toward that end and goal intended by the Gospel.

The eschatological church is merely the church as originally intended. Where this fact is lost or denied, the church withers, exchang-ing eternal realities for temporal and material replacements that, in the end, are incapable of giving life. But the eschatological church is a revived, renewed and reformed church. It is a church anchored in the past and future, in the historic Jesus who will return and who, at this very moment, is preparing his bride for the wedding feast of the Lamb. To be an eschatological church is to know and enjoy the presence of God – Father, Son, and Holy Spirit – in its very midst. It is to be called, consecrated and anointed by this presence and, thus, to exist not as a club, institute or organization, but as his Body, alive and well in him. And by living in his presence, by living out and living in the eschatolog-ical realities given by God, we enter a wholly new reality. The Christian life, attending church, serving and giving become acts eternally valid.

And, in doing them, we find that our lives, bound and hidden in this temporal and fallen order, actually are lived out on the threshold of heaven:

> "You have not come to something that can be touched, a blazing fire, and darkness, and gloom, and a tempest, and the sound of a trumpet, and a voice whose words made the hearers beg that not another word be spoken to them.... But you have come to Mount Zion and to the city of the living God, the heavenly Jerusalem, and to innumerable angels in festal gathering, and to the assembly of the firstborn who are enrolled in heaven, and to God the judge of all, and to the spirits of the righteous made perfect, and to Jesus, the mediator of a new covenant, and to the sprinkled blood that speaks a better word than the blood of Abel."[3]

---

3. Hebrews 12:18-24.

Chapter Seven

REPORT OF THE TASK FORCE
ON PEACE, UNITY AND PURITY

There are many points – great and small – that may be made in
assessing, critiquing and responding to the report from the Theological Task Force on Peace, Unity and Purity.[1] Time and space,
however, allows only a very limited response and critique. The first will
look at the theology section of the report and the second will look
specifically at the task force's fifth recommendation.

Theological Section

At first glance, there appears to be much within the theological section of the report that would commend itself to the evangelical perspective. The prologue is orthodox, Biblical and Reformed, and faithfully
expresses essential aspects of our faith and life. That is not to say, however, that it is without problems, even where essentially orthodox.[2] Nevertheless, its statements are faithful and use vocabulary and concepts
that should be affirmed.

But there are two vast problems in and through the report that render
it a fatally flawed document. The first problem is that the report dis-
guises massive change as no change, and radical transformation as a
return to historic and traditional Presbyterianism. Affirming tradition
and standards, it nevertheless promotes local option for ordination stan-

---

1. Many, of course, have been made and are available through many of the Presbyter-
    ian Web sites.

2. The statements on baptism, for example, are extremely high and reflect more of a
    Roman Catholic perspective than a Reformed one (lines 117-21).

dards that certainly and inevitably will change the church at every level.

The second problem lies not so much in what is said, but in what is not said; not so much in what is explicit, but in what is implicit, tacit and undefined. Words and concepts repeatedly are used without definition. The report begins with three theological axioms, all orthodox and faithful to Scripture, but, at the same time, all controversial and subject to diverse interpretations. To testify that such simple (and true!) axioms as "God loves us" (line 24), God "saves us" (line 25) and God "empowers us with a calling and commission" does not mean that each is understood in identical or even similar ways. The latter elaborations within the report fail to adequately define or shape the terms and, in fact, only further confuse the issue.[3]

The two most important sections – Christology and Scripture – are profoundly problematic. Little actually is given to the church to enlarge and explain its faith and understanding of Christ. The members of the task force assert that they "were inspired by the power of the affirmation 'Jesus is Lord'" (line 502f), without any description or interpretation of what this crucial phrase means and, conversely, does not mean. Stating that they "were instructed by a variety of Christological affirmations that have been accepted as Christian and Reformed" (line 505), the members of the task force leave unanswered huge and pressing questions. Which sources were used? Which were understood as most valid and which as less so and why? While admitting our "tendencies to oversimplify" claims about Jesus within the current debate, the members of the task force make no effort to describe how this actually occurs. Which definitions, from whom and expressing what, are oversimplifications? Ultimately, almost nothing is actually said about Christology. In a report of more than 1,500 lines, remarkably only 34 lines

---

3. Examples abound. The report states that "our savior has pursued us in our way-wardness" without defining "waywardness" (line 44) or (apparently) recognizing that evangelicals and progressives will understand and apply this word in very different ways. Which is intended? The word "lost" (line 45) is Biblical and used by evangelicals and progressives alike, but with very different meanings. We affirm that the love of God destroys alienating distinctions and produces unity, but is this unity an anthropological or soteriological reality (lines 99-101)? Through the whole of the report, and especially through its foundational theological section, terms are used without any definition, clarification or distinction. And because of this, anyone will be able to shape such terms into whatever meaning or purpose he or she intends. Ironically, the very section most esteemed and held up as the uniting hope and belief of the church is, in fact, so vague and unclear as to be all but totally worthless. Filled with faithful and Biblical axioms, these remain impotent and useless without any clear definition and each will, in the end, find definition in the hands of many disparate opinions.

address this essential issue (lines 486-520).

The equally crucial section on Biblical interpretation also lacks any clear direction, definition, or detail. Affirming their own use of Scripture and a study of various methods of Biblical interpretation, the members of the task force fail to recommend any approach or method to the church. They affirm that there are a "variety of models of biblical authority and interpretation" (line 551), without any guidance as to what constitutes valid and faithful interpretation. The authority of Scripture is upheld without any definition as to what authority actually means and how it practically may be used in the conflicts that are destroying our peace, unity and purity. Certainly, the members of the task force would agree that Scripture can be wrongly and rightly interpreted. But nowhere are we provided the guidance and help we need to avoid the former and practice the latter. In the end, the members of the task force only can affirm that Scripture is important and that Presbyterians disagree about how it is to be interpreted. We, of course, knew this before the task force was even formed.

The lack of theological clarity will render the report vapid at the least, but dangerous if good terms are twisted to bear un-Biblical meanings. It is, therefore, incumbent upon the church to carefully define the terms and ideas used in the report and to ensure that they are properly interpreted. Even more boldly, the church needs an alternative statement that clearly articulates in our day and time, in the midst of our crisis and controversy, what it is we believe. We must do more than affirm that God loves us, saves us and empowers us. We must do even more than simply express what these mean. We also must make clear what they do not mean – and cannot mean – if we are to remain faithful to the Gospel.

If peace, unity and purity are to be truly known and enjoyed, we must move beyond mere phrases, however orthodox, and present to the church a clear articulation of what we believe. We must lead the people under our care into a clear understanding of the Gospel, with all that it means and all that it does not mean. We must produce an alternative to this report that actually accomplishes what the Task Force was called to do.

Recommendation Five

Recommendation five, which calls for the adoption of an authoritative interpretation that would allow a governing body to decide whether or not an explicit constitutional standard is an "essential of the Reformed faith and polity," is the crux of the document and the point at which the future of the church will be determined. The bulk of the report, being innocuous and ill-defined, likely will have little impact upon the church. It largely will carry on as before, with each person defining the Gospel and faith as is right in his or her own eyes and interpreting Scripture with all the usual variety and breadth we have come to know. Recommendation five, though, will change the church as we know it.

The language of recommendation five is profoundly misleading. It speaks openly of "national standards" and affirms the right of review by higher governing bodies. Both, however, effectively are annulled – the former by the reality that there are no real national standards and the latter by section five of the recommendation, which limits the propriety of review. The concept of "scruples" has validity when one is asked to affirm a single standard like the Westminster Confession and Catechisms. But the existence of the *Book of Order,* combined with our ordination vows, makes the concept unhelpful and even dangerous. We no longer have any definable standard. We vow to hold to essential tenets without ever knowing what they are, and we promise to be guided by the confessions, whatever exactly that may mean. To affirm the existence and validity of national standards and the right to announce a scruple arguably is meaningless today. Unfortunately, the promise of standards and review likely will assure many people that this recommendation will bring no great change or harm to the church. It's more likely that the opposite is true. Without any real standards and with judicatories that may, but ought not to, review and overturn decisions of ordaining bodies, the recommendation's assurances are rendered anemic and impotent.

The use of the word "any" (line 1197) suggests that, in theory, any point of faith and practice may be placed upon the table as a "scruple" and that any point of doctrine or practice may be considered non-essential. As our church already has demonstrated a profound willingness to redefine doctrine and practice, such official license will allow every session and presbytery to decide for itself what is essential and what is right in its own eyes. On the left, some people no doubt will hold that homosexuality is not essential and is insufficient grounds for denying ordination. On the right, some people no doubt will decide that women's ordination is invalid and will declare as a scruple their unwillingness to ordain or recognize as valid women in ministry. And while any and all decisions may be reviewed, the recommendation (lines 1205-1208) expressly and explicitly encourages the higher judicatories to remain uninvolved, trusting that the ordaining body made a right and faithful decision. In spite of claims to the contrary, this is nothing less than local option and, as such, is a denial of Presbyterian practice and tradition from the church's earliest days.

The recommendation is dangerous because of its power. An authoritative interpretation has constitutional authority and force. That means it will have the power of law in its exact wording. And it is only the exact wording that will have this power and force. All rationale and intentions (lines 1212-1456) effectively will be lost as decisions made by various judicatories and Permanent Judicial Commissions will be limited to the strict and precise wording of the authoritative interpretation.

This recommendation renders the report as a whole a schismatic document. That is not to say or even imply that was the intent of the task force or its members. Indeed, it most certainly was not. But if this recommendation is received and practiced, there will be no unity and no peace within the church. Every ordination will be a potential conflict, every transfer from one presbytery to another will be grounds for a rigid, pressing examination. Each presbytery and session will be able to do what is right in its own eyes. And any appeal to national standards, when these essentially are undefined and uncertain, would be meaningless.

Chapter Eight

Recommendations
Essential Tenets and a Confessional Church

The Presbyterian Church (USA) is a confessional church. That is, from its start and through the whole of its history, it has affirmed that there exist teachings, concepts and interpretations that are an essential and necessary part of the church's life and faith. Conversely, as the flip side of this truth, the church has held that there also exist false ideas, untruths and errors that must be noted, condemned and corrected.

The confessing of the faith has occurred through three primary means: the proper interpretation of Scripture; its systematic articulation in theology, creeds and confessions; and its proclamation through the preaching of the Word. This threefold confessional form goes back to John Calvin who, through his commentaries, *The Institutes* and other theological writings and the preaching of the Word, sought to regularly, clearly and faithfully confess the faith of the church. This confessional nature is a defining characteristic of the Presbyterian Church (USA). That we are a confessing church is undeniable. What this means and what precisely it is that we confess is less clear. The evangelical wing of the church has sought to maintain the church's confessional nature from the very birth of the Reformed faith. And the maintenance of this confessional natures means more than the mere critical reception advocated by the church's progressive wing. To confess the faith, to be a confessing church, is to acknowledge that there are, and have been since the birth of the church, truths and realities that are unchanging and, conversely, do not change across time, culture and popular whim.

In this time of ambiguity, tension and division, it is essential that the church more precisely define its faith and confession. It is time to affirm and confess, with both clarity and conviction, what it means to be the church and what is expected of our members and leaders. It is time to accept, define and articulate some essential tenets. I suggest

that, without at least basic tenets, our vows are meaningless and our
future dubious. I suggest, on the most practical level, that the church
accept and declare basic tenets of faith and practice that are required of
all in ordained office and membership within the Presbyterian Church
(USA). There are many forms these may take, and the following is submitted as one that has proven profoundly useful over the last two years.

Faith and Membership[1]

"Are you tired? Worn out? Burned out on religion? Come to Me. Get
away with me and you'll recover your life. I'll show you how to take a
real rest. Walk with me and work with me ... keep company with me
and you'll learn to live freely and lightly."

Jesus, Matthew 11 (*The Message*)

Just as Christ Jesus welcomes all, so we in the Presbyterian Church
(USA) welcome and invite all to participate in worship, study, fellowship, prayer and to receive pastoral care. Whether a person is a seeker or
devout, broken or healed, grieving or rejoicing, all are free to join us in
our quest to seek, learn and enjoy our God and to know the love and
support of the church.

While participation in any or all of these areas is open to all, without
restriction, definition, or limitation,[2] active membership is more carefully and precisely defined in the Presbyterian Church (USA). Every
Christian church is entitled and expected to declare the terms of admis-
sion into its communion[3] and describe the nature, content and look of
faith expected of its members. It is crucial, therefore, that the meaning
of faith, discipleship and membership clearly is defined and understood
within the church.

"One becomes an active member of the church through faith in Jesus
Christ and acceptance of his Lordship in all of life"[4]

The church is God's creation and work. We believe that the Father,
from the creation of the human race, faithfully has preserved, instructed,
multiplied, honored, adored, and called from death to life a gathering of
faithful people.[5] We affirm that God was in Christ, reconciling the world

---

1. The following section is taken from the standards required for membership at
    Community Presbyterian Church in Ventura, California.

2. G-5.0301, *Book of Order*, part II.

3. G-1.0302, *Book of Order*, part II.

4. G-5.0101, *Book of Order*, part II.

5. 3.05, *Book of Confessions*, part I.

to himself, making us his new creation, and calling us to be ambassadors of reconciliation[6] and witnesses to the transforming power of Christ's resurrection. As such, the church exists as the Body of Christ,[7] a people of integrity, purity and devotion, born of God and ceaselessly striving to faithfully respond to the faithfulness of our Father in heaven. We are, by God's gracious work, a people of faith.

Faith in Jesus Christ is the only basis for church membership and, thus, active membership[8] means nothing less than genuine, vibrant faith in Christ that accepts and exhibits his Lordship over all of life. By our faith, we are justified; that is, declared righteous in His eyes and reconciled to God. Thus, faith provides an understanding of God's nature, will and work, binds us in trusting relationship to the Lord, and defines the shape of our lives. For these reasons, the health of the church and its members is directly tied to the depth, integrity and truth of the faith they hold and live.

We understand faith to be "the sure and certain knowledge of God's benevolence toward us, which, being founded on the truth of the gracious promise in Christ, is both revealed to our minds and confirmed in our hearts by the Holy Spirit."[9] Faith is not an opinion, perspective or feeling. It is more than mere personal conviction. Faith is the fruit and effect of the Holy Spirit's work on our lives. Revealing the truth of God to our hearts, the Spirit enables us to see and comprehend God's will and enables us to wholeheartedly follow and live a life that is pleasing to God.

We hold that faith means nothing less than understanding, receiving and appropriately responding to the essential tenets of the Christian faith; that is, the real acts and revealed nature and, thus, the truth of God our Father. These are learned from the Bible's witness, expressed in our confessions and include[10] our affirmation:

---

6. 2 Corinthians 5:17-21.

7. See Rom. 7:4, 12:5; I Cor. 12:27; Eph. 4:12, 5:23. See also 5.130, 6.054, 6.186, *The Book of Confessions*, part I; and G-1.0100, *Book of Order*, part II.

8. G-5.0103, *Book of Order*, part II.

9. John Calvin, *Institutes of The Christian Religion*, III.ii.7. See also 5.112, *Book of Confessions*, part I.

10. This should not be considered an exhaustive list of all that one might include as an "essential tenet." This simply notes some crucial points of faith that have been held by the church across its whole history, proclaimed in the Scriptures and affirmed in the creeds and confessions of the Presbyterian Church (USA). The Scriptures and *The Book of Confessions* provide a fuller and richer understanding of the content, object and meaning of faith.

- ... of the Trinity and God's existence as one being in three persons, Father, Son, and Holy Spirit.
- .... of the Lordship of Jesus.
- ... of Jesus Christ's dual nature, fully God and fully human.
- ... that Jesus suffered under Pontius Pilate, was crucified, dead, and buried.
- ... of the forgiveness of sins through faith in the person and work of Christ.
- ... of Jesus' bodily resurrection from the dead and ascension to heaven.
- ... that salvation is through Christ alone.
- ... that salvation is by grace through faith, not of works.

- ... of the person and work of the Holy Spirit, who with the Father and the Son works to effect our salvation.
- ... of the Bible's divine inspiration and authority over all matters of faith and life.
- ... that God has, through Christ, called a church into being to do His will and proclaim his nature and work.
- ... that we are to live holy lives after the example of Christ.
- ... that we are to go into all the world, making disciples of all people and teaching them all that Jesus said and did.
- ... that Jesus will return to gather his church to himself and reign forever over all creation.

Faith as Response

Active membership is a specific response of faith by which we publicly submit the whole of our lives to the Lordship of Christ, entrust the whole of our lives to his mercy and grace, live the whole of our lives in joyous expectant obedience, and give the whole of our lives to the manifestation, exhibition and expansion of his kingdom. Most practically, active membership means personal commitment to and sharing in the proclamation of the good news; participation in the life and worship of the church; prayer; study of the Scriptures and faith of the church; and supporting the church through the giving of money, time, support, and service.[11] Faith informs and transforms our lives – knowing and trusting God's will and work, we are justified (declared righteous) and, living our faith before God and under the guidance of the Holy Spirit, we are sanctified (made righteous). In faith, we turn to God and, in the process, turn from all that would keep us from him and his blessings.

> "Since, then, we do not have the excuse of ignorance, everything – and I do mean everything – connected with that old way of life has to go. It's rotten through and through. Get rid of it! And then take on an entirely new way of life – a God-fashioned life, a life renewed from the

---

11. G-5.0102, *Book of Order*, part II.

inside and working itself into your conduct as God accurately repro-
duces his character in you. What this adds up to, then, is this: no more
lies, no more pretense.... In Christ's body we're all connected to each
other, after all."[12]

We hold that faith in Christ and purity of life are the two necessary
sides of the one act of Christian discipleship. One cannot have one without the other.[13] Jesus came that we might have life, and have it abun-
dantly.[14] This means that faith not only receives God's gifts and blessings, it endeavors to throw off all that would limit, deny or annul them,
whether in ourselves or in others. Faith and, thus, church membership is
to put off the old and put on the new life God intends and, thus, as an
act of faith, in obedience and love to God, and in pursuit of that life
Christ came to give, we put off our sinful nature seeking to reflect the
image of Christ Jesus.

Marks of the sinful nature[15]

- Sexual immorality: adultery, impurity, fornication, homosexual
  behavior, lust, pornography, orgies, prostitution, carousing, lewd-
  ness.

- Malice: slander, deceit, murder, bitterness, falsehood, dissension,
  gossip, discord, revenge, hatred, unwholesome talk, coarse joking,
  obscenities, abusive talk, strife, disobedience to parents, treach-
  ery.

- Greed: envy, love of money, theft, jealousy, idolatry, covetousness,
  swindling.

- Lack of self-discipline: fits of rage, drunkenness, debauchery,
  laziness, love of pleasure.

- Pride: selfish ambition, arrogance, boasting, conceit.

- False spirituality: witchcraft, false teaching, empty religion.

---

12. Ephesians 4.22-25 (The Message)

13. Romans 6:1-23; 1 Corinthians 6:9-11; Galatians 2:20; 5:13-18; Ephesians 4:17-
    24; Colossians 2:11-12; 3:1-3; Titus 2:11-3.8; 1 Peter 1:13-2.12; 4:1-7.

14. John 10:10.

15. These are composite lists derived from the following moral/ethical summaries in
    the New Testament: Mark 7:21-23; Romans 1:26-32; 13:8-14; 1 Corinthians 6:9-
    11; Galatians 5:16-21; Ephesians 4:22-5:21; Colossians 3:1-17; 1 Timothy 6:3-10;
    2 Timothy 3:1-9; Hebrews 12:14-13; James 3:14-16; 1 Peter 2:1-3; 4:1-7.

Marks of the new life in Christ

- Sexual purity: fidelity to marital vows between a man and a woman, chastity in singleness.

- Love: honesty, peacemaking, speaks truth in love, forgiving, a mastered tongue, self-control, patience, kindness, sincere, impartial, merciful, considerate, forbearing, compassionate, thankful, loyal, gentle.

- Humility: regard for authority, submissive.

- Freedom from greed: contentment, faithful stewardship, financial/vocational integrity, generosity.

- Sound doctrine: passion for godliness, worshipper of the true God, lover of the Truth.

Not one of us is free from sin, not one of us is perfect[16] and, thus, we all are ever in need of God's grace and forgiveness, which is available to all who confess their sins.[17] We also ever are in need of the loving guidance and support of the church, recognizing that Scripture teaches us to rescue and restore one another in love.[18] Only together, in humility and confession, in the fullness of mutual encouragement and love, growth and prayer, can we grow into the life that Christ died to provide.

We hold that these essential tenets of theology and basic ethical response are necessary components of a Biblical and Reformed faith.

Leadership and Ordination Standards

The Scriptures nowhere teach that there is one standard or expectation for members and another for leaders. There is, through the whole of the New Testament, a clear theological and ethical standard expected of all believers. Leaders are not called to a higher or different ethic, but to the same faith and ethic lived consistently. Thus, it is essential that these standards be carefully and passionately maintained by all in leadership and that the leadership of the church exhibit and teach them to all whom we lead and shepherd.

Proclamation of the Gospel in Times of Controversy

It is the maintenance of and faithfulness to these standards in times

---

16. Romans 3:23, 3:10-18; 1 John 1:8-10; Ecclesiastes 7:20.

17. 1 John 1:5-2.6

18. Matthew 18:15-20; Galatians 6:1-2; James 5:19-20.

of controversy, persecution and/or heresy that the church exhibits her faith and proclaims the Gospel. We do not seek, hope or ask for times of peace so that the Gospel may be proclaimed, but recognize that it is our life, standards and integrity that allow the Gospel to manifest itself within adversity. In every age, controversy and conflict arise that test the church's faith and threaten to diminish or annul her message. In the time of Athanasius, controversies regarding the nature and person of Christ and the Trinity threatened the church's understanding of God's very being. During the Reformation, controversy swirled around and enveloped issues of salvation and how one was made and declared right before God. In our day, we are faced with issues and controversies equally as huge and life threatening. At issue are not peripheral opinions, but matters that touch the essence of what we hold to be true about God, our faith and ourselves. It is, therefore, time for the Presbyterian Church (USA) to rise in defense of the Gospel.

Final/Summary Recommendations

Because "truth is in order to goodness" and our Reformed tradition affirms the necessary connection between faith and practice, theory and lifestyle, we make the following recommendations based upon the Scriptures and our theology:

1. Peace, unity and purity begin with us. We in the network of renewal, within and under the evangelical faith and witness of our church, first and foremost must model peace, unity and purity. Sadly, too often this has been missed as brothers and sisters within our family, and holding to essentially the same theological convictions, nevertheless have engaged in fighting, scolding and shunning one another. We call for a unified response to the heresy before us.

2. Choose this day whom you will follow. For much of the current debate, the majority of the church has remained quiet and uninvolved. We must persuade the "muddy middle" of the importance of these issues and lead them into the truth as well as peace, unity and purity.

3. Essential tenets must be affirmed, maintained and protected by the church at every level and judicatory. This would include sessions, presbyteries, synods, the General Assembly, Permanent Judicial Commissions, etc. The standards of faith and practice described above are neither new to the church nor narrowly held but, on the contrary, exist as standards across the whole of the church regardless of time, place and culture. The diversity and plurality of the age requires the church to make, maintain and adhere to those standards that reflect and maintain its faith.

4. The larger church must encourage the General Assembly to receive, but not adopt, the report of the Theological Task Force on Peace, Unity and Purity. That is, the General Assembly acknowledges the task force's work and conclusions without implementing them. To this end, overtures to the General Assembly should be encouraged.

5. Those who reject the historic tenets of the catholic and Reformed church are invited to peaceably withdraw from the Presbyterian Church (USA). Harsh sounding, perhaps, but it nevertheless is a constitutional option given to the church as a means of promoting peace and furthering its message.

We are in a time of profound crisis. No simple answer will heal our wounds and restore our common life and unity. But there is hope in Christ, who alone is Lord of the church. It is time, perhaps more so than at any other time in her history, for the Presbyterian Church (USA) to affirm clearly what we hold true and good. It is time to take a stand for truth, even at the risk of offending the world. Christ Jesus is both the hope of the world and its chief point of offense and scandal. We cannot have one without the other and, thus, some degree of conflict is inevitable. This is beyond our power to affect or change. But what we can do is remain faithful and true to our God and his work of redemption in Christ Jesus. Ultimately, this is what is at stake. Indeed, it is all that is at stake.

AFTERWORD

CAN THESE BONES LIVE?

"Thou hast made us for thyself, O Lord, and our hearts are restless 'till they find their rest in Thee."

St. Augustine's prayer winds its way across the centuries, finding a voice today among restless denominations that seek peace, unity and purity.

Malpractitioners from a baseless culture prescribe palliatives, but the splintering that threatens mainline denominations in Western Europe and North America will not be cured by quackery. We have been shattered by something profoundly theological, culminating in our responses to one question: "Who do you say that I am?"

Unwilling to answer that question, we look to our feelings, assuming that the restlessness that plagues us comes from within. False physicians have told us that somewhere inside ourselves – if we just dig deeply enough – we can recover our corporate self-esteem. Thus, theology turns to therapy, and we exchange the cross for a couch.

That technique – like peeling the layers of an onion in search of its core – takes us nowhere. Each layer reveals merely another until, at the heart of the matter, we find no substance at all. Is it a wonder that Camus committed suicide, and Sartre stabbed his hand when facing the futility of mere existence? Any search for the self that turns in upon itself is doomed to depression and, ultimately, to death. We are not – and never can be – the source of our salvation, for there is no health in us, certainly nothing that has the power to save.

St. Augustine learned that he would not find respite for his restlessness inside the self. We find ourselves, he finally confessed, "in Thee." It is Revelation, not reason, that ultimately points us to the way, the truth and the life.

This reality, experienced in billions upon billions of personal conversions to Christ over the ages, is equally applicable to today's moribund ecclesiastical institutions. Denominations that want to be healed will find themselves "in Thee."

Therein lies the flaw in the report of the Theological Task Force on Peace, Unity and Purity in the Presbyterian Church (USA). Unwilling to look beyond itself, the task force merely celebrated own existence. Purportedly representing diverse ideologies, its members made much over the fact that they had forged friendships without forfeiting convictions. None of us changed our minds, they declared, but we found a way to be together.

The task force theme was that relationships trump theology. No one can question or demean the claim of the members that they learned to love one another, but what shall one make of such a claim, other than to say that, as a theological statement, it has no meaning?

Not only is the task force's report unhelpful, it is dangerous. Choosing the task force's theology (all ideas must be honored) and its methodology (yes/no questions are to receive both/and answers), plunges us into pluralism. Declaring that all ideas are equal does not promote peace, unity and purity. Rather, it suggests that a theological question can be answered by politics, a suggestion that undermines the integrity of the Gospel.

The two pastor-theologians whose work is encompassed in this volume offer a Biblically-faithful response to the assignment that the task force failed to fulfill. Together, they share a gift with the church that does, in fact, chart a course toward the church's peace, unity and purity. They do so by beginning, not with an exploration of themselves, but with Scripture, the Word of God.

Gerrit Scott Dawson reminds us that peace, unity and purity are not human accomplishments, but gifts from the Triune God of grace. In the exquisite harmony of Father, Son and Holy Spirit, that loving interaction of three divine persons in eternal communion, we see the peace, unity and purity that we seek. As we are drawn into that Trinitarian presence, we experience something that in our brokenness we never could have achieved. The church's participation in that Holy Communion is its peace, unity and purity.

Mark R. Patterson reminds us that there is a world of difference between spirituality and theology. Spirituality is nothing more than the human search for meaning, connection, a place in the cosmos. Spirituality is an experience that begins and ends with ourselves. Theology, on the other hand, begins with Theos. From beginning to end, theology is all about God.

The task force's failed precisely because it did not honor this distinction between spirituality and theology. One finds a sense of commonality in its discussions, for humans of every stripe pursue a spiritual quest. But there is nothing in sharing our spirituality that leads us beyond ourselves.

Central to Patterson's work is the doctrine of grace. He tells us that grace is not "an abstract principle," "an ambivalent acceptance of any and all," "a benign tolerance." Grace always encompasses a "no" to our sin, even as it pronounces a "yes" to our salvation. Grace and the judgment of a holy God are inseparable.

In the task force's desire to maintain fellowship among disparate worldviews and behaviors, it sacrificed the "no" that must be confronted before we can hear the "yes." In fact, by urging the church to avoid yes/no dichotomies, the task force's report actually leads people away from God's grace.

Dawson and Patterson encourage the church to eschew such language, for it is derived from a culture that does not know Christ. They warn us of an alien atmosphere, an air that is not fit to breathe, that will fill our lungs with poison, deflate our spirits, and drive us to despair. They urge the church to breathe the pure air of the Gospel.

Mere opinions pooled by the members of the task force, however well-meaning and sincere, are unable to engender new life. Patterson calls on Presbyterians to recover and reclaim essential truths of Christian faith, verities that are founded in nothing less than the Word of God. Dawson urges individuals and members of sessions to exhale culture's poisonous air while seeking inspiration from Word of God.

Scripture's interchangeable use of the words "wind" and "breath" and "Spirit" are instructive here. On the day of our birth, the Creator breathed into our nostrils the breath of life, and we became living beings. On the day of Pentecost, the Word of the Lord was preached and a mighty wind stirred God's people, filling them with lively faith, the courage to proclaim it, and the means to voice it in every tongue. It is noteworthy that God's Word refers to itself as "inspired" (God breathed).

Can these bones live? Ezekiel contemplated that question while facing the bone yard of a bygone faith. The prophet was commissioned to proclaim the Word of the Lord before that calcified congregation. He did so, and a mighty wind began to move among the bones. Filled with the Spirit that inevitably accompanies God's Word, a broken Israel found healing, and new life flourished among God's people.

Can these bones live? The history of God's interaction with his people tells us that they can. But first we must hear his Word:

"If my people who are called by my name humble themselves, and pray and seek my face and turn from their wicked ways, then I will hear from heaven and will forgive their sin and heal their land."[1]

Parker T. Williamson
Lenoir, North Carolina

---

1.   2 Chronicles 7:14.

APPENDIX

Appendix

TABLE OF CONTENTS

Given and Sent in One Love

The True Church of Jesus Christ
A Study Guide

GIVEN AND SENT IN ONE LOVE
THE TRUE CHURCH OF JESUS CHRIST

A STUDY GUIDE

Distribute copies of *Given and Sent in One Love: The True Church of Jesus Christ* to all participants at least one week prior to the first study. Invite them to read both *Given and Sent in One Love* and John 17 prior to the first study session. All participants should bring the book and their Bibles to the study.

Follow one of two tracks: Six weekly, one-hour meetings or two, three-hour meetings.

Chapter One and Chapter Two

a) After opening with prayer, read aloud John 16:29-17:6.

b) Discuss: What time in Jesus' life did he say these things? What seems to be his principle concern as he begins his prayer?

c) What does it mean that the disciples were given to Jesus by his Father? What is it Jesus desires to give to those who were given to him?

d) How does Jesus define eternal life in John 17:3?

e) Read aloud Chapter Two: The Nature of the Church: The Gift of the Triune God.

f) How can the life of the Triune God be understood as a love story?

g) What is the place of human beings in this Triune love story?

h) How is the Church the gift of the Father to the Son? How is the Church the gift of the Son to the Father? How is the Church the gift of the Spirit to the Father and the Son?

i) How is the Church (1) the body of Christ; (2) the temple of Christ; and (3) the bride of Christ? How do these images fit in with the Triune love story?

j) What value is placed on us as part of the Church as those given in love by the Father, Son and Holy Spirit to each other?

k) Look again at the four bullet points in Chapter Two about what the Church is not. What do those points have to say about the present discussions people are having about the nature of the Church?

Chapter Three: The Peace of the Church

a) After opening with prayer, read aloud John 16:16-22.

b) Discuss: What were the disciples not understanding? What did Jesus say would be the basis for their unshakeable joy?

c) Read aloud John 16:32. What does Jesus mean by "the world?" What is the basis for the peace of the disciples?

d) Read aloud John 17: 8-19. What does Jesus pray will be the relationship between the disciples and the world?

e) Read aloud Chapter Three. In the third paragraph, how is the "world" defined?

f) Why does remaining "agnostic," or "without definite knowledge," protect the autonomy of the individual self?

g) How do you see people today retreating into phrases such as, "Well, we can't really know anything definite about God," in order to avoid conflict, decline the hard work of theological thought, or to preserve their private beliefs?

h) How does the story of Jesus that occurred in the space and time of our real world "assault" such agnosticism?

i) Discuss the five stages in the history of Jesus' arrivals and departures found on p. 33. Has Jesus-history concluded? Why?

j) Given the definition of the world and the story of Jesus, why must the Church ever be in conflict with the world?

k) Why do we nevertheless go to the world with the story of Jesus? How does John 3:16 inform your answer?

l) What is our peace in the midst of this conflict?

m) Discuss the four points on p. 34 related to who Jesus is not. What do those points have to say to the present discussions people are having about the person and Lordship of Jesus?

Chapter Four: The Purity of the Church

a) After beginning with prayer, read aloud John 17:14-19.

b) Discuss: What does it mean to sanctify? Are their other translations of that word in John 17:17?

c) Sanctify can mean to consecrate, to cleanse, to purify, to set apart for a sacred purpose. What connection does Jesus make between the truth and being sanctified?

d) In John 17:17, what does Jesus equate with truth? What is the Father's word? How does the Word of God set us apart, purify us, with truth?

e) Read aloud Chapter Four: The Purity of the Church.

f) What does this chapter assert is the great danger today to the peace of the church in the Presbyterian Church (USA)?

g) In the quotation from Lesslie Newbigin on p. 38, how does the Church's separation *from* the world affect the mission of the Church *to* the world?

h) How, then, does the purity of the Church affect its peace?

i) From p. 40, why is it not arrogance to confess the truth?

j) What is the difference between *comprehending* everything about God and *apprehending* the true knowledge about God's revelation in Christ?

k) How does Deuteronomy 29:29 address the question of truth and humility in the Church?

Chapter Five: The Unity of the Church

a) After beginning with prayer, read aloud John 17:11, 20-26. How is the unity of the Church connected to the unity of the Father and the Son?

b) How does our demonstration of unity affect the world's perception of who Jesus is?

c) If the world, which is essentially hostile to God, is to *know* Christ the Savior of the world, what must the Church be and do?

d) Read aloud Chapter Five: The Unity of the Church.

e) Discuss: How does the chapter say our union in Christ is related to our union with one another?

f) What is the relationship between submission to the truth of Christ and our union with each other?

g) What makes consecrated unity in Christ and the struggle in our denomination so crucial to our witness to the world?

h) Discuss the half-truth phrase from p. 45, "Unity means we must accept people with whom we differ, even people whom we dislike." What is true in that statement? How can the statement be used erroneously?

i) Discuss the half-truth phrase from p. 46, "They label as heretics anyone who does not agree with them, anyone who does not accept their narrow, fundamentalist expression of faith." What is true in that statement? How can the statement be used erroneously?

j) Discuss the half-truth phrase from p. 46, "What matters most is that we all just get along." What is true in that statement? How can the statement be used erroneously?

k) Discuss the half-truth phrase from p. 47, "We must not impose our Western, middle class values on others." What is true in that statement? How can the statement be used erroneously?

l) How does the Triune God create unity in the Church?

Chapter Six: The Alien Atmosphere
Our Denomination Breathes

a) After beginning with prayer, read aloud Ephesians 2:1-5. What do you think Paul means by "the ruler of the power of the air?" How do you discern the "air" or "atmosphere" of a family, group, company, church, or even nation? What concrete signs tell you what the "air" is like?

b) What descriptions does Paul give of the "air" of our former lives outside of Christ in the world?

c) Read aloud I Thessalonians 1:9-10. What distinction does Paul make between a life outside of Christ and a life in Christ?

d) Read aloud I Peter 2:9-12. How are we now strangers and aliens in the world?

e) Read aloud Chapter Six: The Alien Atmosphere Our Denomination Breathes.

f) Discuss: What is the normal Biblical "atmosphere" regarding sexual ethics?

g) Has American culture over the past decades been moving closer or further from Biblical values? If you said further, should the Church then look more or less like the culture today? Does the PC(USA) look sharply distinct from our culture or more like a mirror of culture?

h) What do you make of Phillip Turner's distinction between the official theology of a denomination and its working theology? What would you say is the working theology prevalent in the PC(USA)?

i) In the list of 10 questions on pp. 53-55, which strike you more as "liberal" or "progressive" sins and which strike you more as "conservative" or "evangelical" sins?

j) Which do you find most disturbing? Which do you find most convicting?

k) Discuss the "deep, simple truths" in the five bullet points on pp. 55-56. Are these affirmations you or your session could make?

Chapter Seven and Eight: A Call to Faithful Action Based on Acts 15-16

a) After beginning with prayer, read aloud Acts 15:1-16:5.

b) What was the debate about in the early church? What was at stake in this issue of keeping the law? How might the "Judaizers" be "troubling" the church?

c) How did the apostles determine the right course of action? What decision did they make? What were the essentials they decreed? How did they make the decision known? What is effective about face-to-face contact?

d) What was the result in the churches of the apostolic proclamation? How do authoritative boundaries serve to increase the faith and numbers of the Church?

e) Read aloud Chapter Seven: A Call to Faithful Action Based on Acts 15-16.

f) Discuss: What burdens are placed on our churches by the theological "innovations" being advanced in the PC(USA)? (Four are described on pp. 57-58).

g) What effect might a strong, Biblical stance from a General Assembly have on our congregations? What do the voices from the world church say to us?

h) Read aloud Chapter Eight: Going to Declare Truth.

i) What feelings are evoked when you consider going to another individual or session to bear witness to the truth you hold?

j) Discuss: Could your session go through the process of creating a list of essential aspects of the truth? Could your session spend time in prayerful repentance as part of this process?

k) Read aloud the Guide for Sessions Visiting Other Sessions in Appendix Two.

l) Are there those on the session who would be willing to be part of a team to visit other churches? Which other sessions do you feel called to address?

m) If your session will take this challenge, work toward determining your list of essential aspects, either by beginning the process or scheduling a time to do so.

Appendix Two

A Guide for Sessions Visiting Other Sessions

A Guide for Sessions
Affirming and Declaring the Truth
In Visits to Other Sessions

1. Study *Given and Sent in One Love: The True Church of Jesus Christ*, using the study guide provided. We recommend meeting together weekly for six, one-hour meetings. Or meet for two, three-hour periods.

2. Next, as a session, identify those aspects of the truth concerning Christ and his Church that you consider to be essential. There are many such essential aspects listed in the book. You also may find excellent summaries in such documents as the Presbyterian Coalition's Union in Christ (http://www.presbycoalition.org/union.htm), the Essentials Tenets of the New Wineskins Movement, (http://www.presbywine.com/2004/09/essential_tenet.html) or the essential tenets adopted by the Presbytery of San Diego (http://www.presbyterysd.org/reports/etrdmaster.pdf). You also might review the 1978 General Assembly's Authoritative Interpretation (http://www.presbycoalition.org/authint.htm). We suggest working with a chart pad or Power Point program to first put up a large number of aspects. Then, work to hone your list to six to 10 essentials that relate to the present situation in our denomination. Be sure your list reflects aspects of the truth that always have been part of the Christian witness and that are non-negotiable for you. Consider making your list a session resolution to be shared with the congregation and which expresses your faith for the present situation of the PC(USA).

3. Consider how the truth concerning Christ and his Church expressed in this book and in your list of essentials (a) affirms your faith and work as a session; (b) convicts your session of ways in which you have failed the truth (the list of ten bracing questions in Chapter Six should provide sufficient conviction for all of us); and (c) what steps of repentance you will take as a session.

4. Identify a team of elders willing to visit other sessions (three-to-five elders would make a reasonable size group). The pastor may be included, but we suggest that he or she not be the primary spokesperson. On that team, identify both a primary spokesperson, who will present your convictions, and a recorder, who will keep a record of the questions and responses raised by your visit.

5. Identify six PC(USA) congregations in your presbytery with whom you would like to share your convictions and your confessions.

6. Your Clerk of Session then will call the clerks in the six congregations you have identified, asking for a 30-minute appointment with their sessions. We suggest saying something such as, "We would like to send a team of our elders to visit with your session to share what is on our hearts concerning our faith and the situation of our denomination."

7. Before each meeting, your team should gather for much prayer, and to review your talking points.

8. During your visit to another session, be gracious and humble, thanking them for the opportunity to share the convictions most dear to you. Ask if you may pray before you begin.

9. Your spokesperson will share your list of essential aspects of the truth, quietly and humbling declaring the truth of Christ and his Church as it relates to where we are as a denomination. You might prepare a handout with your essentials on it in outline form. Other members of the team should be in silent prayer during the sharing of information.

10. In concert with your declaration, share how these essentials have brought your own session under conviction, and in what ways you have repented. Conclude by issuing an invitation to that session to join you in repentance before the truth of Christ and his Church.

11. Listen humbly and politely to the response from the members of the other session, and answer their questions as best you can. Let other team members answer questions or make responses so that the spokesperson does not become the sole focus of the discussion.

12. Do not engage in debate. These essentials are not debatable for you. You simply want to share them with the members of the other session. Do not engage in a protracted discussion. The purpose is to declare truth, offer confession and invite repentance.

13. Do not agree that "we just see things differently," or that "there are

many valid ways to interpret the Scriptures about these matters." You have come humbly to say that, "This is the truth of the historic Church and outside that truth is error."

14. Keep your visit brief, in the range of half an hour. Have someone on your team watch the time and be bold to make your exit before too much time passes.

15. Meet to debrief and pray afterward.

16. Remember that witness to the truth is powerful. Its effects may not be seen in the moment. The immediate reactions may not be positive, but the long-term results may be great.

17. Share the results from each visit at your session meetings.

18. At the conclusion of your visits, spend an hour at your session's meeting discussing what you have learned, what you see as the future of the PC(USA), and what next steps you might be led to take.

Appendix Three

AN ANALYSIS

THE REPORT OF THE THEOLOGICAL TASK FORCE ON PEACE, UNITY AND PURITY IN THE PRESBYTERIAN CHURCH (USA)

Editor's Note

The Theological Task Force on Peace, Unity and Purity (USA) was created by the 213th General Assembly (2001) "to lead the Presbyterian Church (USA) in spiritual discernment of our Christian identity in and for the 21st century..." (Minutes, 2001, Part I, p. 29).

Its 17 members, comprised to reflect the theological and cultural diversity of the denomination, were directed to lead the Presbyterian Church (USA) in "spiritual discernment of our Christian identity, in and for the 21st century, using a process which includes conferring with synods, presbyteries, and congregations seeking the peace, unity and purity of the church. This discernment shall include but not be limited to issues of Christology, biblical authority and interpretation, ordination standards, and power."

The task force released its final report September 15, 2005, and it will be considered June 15-22, 2006, by the 217th General Assembly when it meets in Birmingham, Alabama. It is available online at www.pcusa.org/peaceunitypurity.

This analysis of the task force's report, prepared by the Presbyterian Lay Committee, examines, in turn, the theological and methodological, governance and polity considerations underlying the report. It then offers conclusions based on that examination.

The analysis includes references to line numbers in the task force's report, so as to provide an easy-to-use format applicable as a study guide for individuals, small groups, sessions and presbyteries.

TABLE OF CONTENTS

Editor's Note: The numbers in parentheses – (line 1150), for example – refer to the line number of the report of the Theological Task Force on the Peace, Unity and Purity of the Presbyterian Church (USA).

I. Theological and Methodological Considerations

F. The process utilized in generating the report is proffered to the General Assembly of the Presbyterian Church (USA) as a model for replication among all governing bodies. This process, based on a group's self-consciousness rather than Scripture, is deeply flawed.

II. Governance and Polity Considerations

A. The task force report's recommendation would repeal the Authoritative Interpretation already issued by the General Assembly Permanent Judicial Commission that states the relation of G-6.0106b and G-6.0108 in the *Book of Order*; namely, that G-6.0106b overrides any ordaining body's discretion in determining standards for the sexual behavior of persons to be ordained.

B. The task force report's recommendation would violate the understanding of the constitutional process for change reached by the Special Commission of 1925 with respect to setting ordination standards.

C. The task force report's recommendation would adopt a "presumption of wisdom" in favor of the ordaining body that would be all but impossible to be overcome in any review by higher governing bodies (lines 1199-1206). Thus, in reality, the decision of the ordaining body regarding whether a standard was an "essential" would be final.

D. The task force report's recommendation would allow the standards of sexual behavior based on at least 2,000 years of Biblical understanding to be violated by ordaining bodies pending an indeterminate process of discernment (lines 1353-1356).

E. The task force report recommends that the General Assembly "direct" and "urge" governing bodies to "explore the use of alternative forms of discernment and decision-making ..." (line 1150). This recommendation is tantamount to a *de facto* amendment to the *Book of Order*.

I. Theological and Methodological Considerations

"Peace if possible. Truth at all costs"

Martin Luther

A. The content of the task force report, when taken as a whole, violates a constitutional principle of church order; namely, that "no opinion can be either more pernicious or more absurd than that which brings truth and falsehood upon a level, and represents it as of no consequence what a man's opinions are. On the contrary, we are persuaded that there is an inseparable connection between faith and practice, truth and duty. Otherwise, it would be of no consequence either to discover truth or to embrace it" (*Book of Order* G-1.0304).

1) The task force declares that it has found "unity" by engaging in a process wherein "we have come to respect the integrity with which theological views different from our own are held, and we have seen that many others in the church have the same capacity to perceive the biblical basis and Christian credibility of other perspectives" (line 1071).

2) The task force declares that, in its process of discernment, it has discovered how to be "moved and impressed by the depth and truth of statements made by our colleagues," (line 399) and that it is able to affirm unity, even though its members "have not compromised our basic convictions or commitments" (line 414).

3) The task force recommends that "all parties should endeavor to outdo one another in honoring one another's decisions ..." (line 1204).

4) The task force suggests that discerning between the truth and falsehood of contrasting positions should be disparaged as "fostering alienation" (lines 193-197).

5) The task force argues against debate, wherein contradictory

positions are identified. It calls this procedure "stereotyping" and "placing labels" (lines 342-382).

6) These statements and recommendations, replete throughout the report from beginning to end, reveal the essence of the task force's methodology that it proffers to the church; namely, that a wide variety of "views," "perspectives," "theologies," "core convictions," – even mutually contradictory beliefs in which the affirmation of one would necessarily mean the denial of the other – can be affirmed, honored, respected, and held together within one ecclesiastical institution. This leads to the nonsensical proposition that any sincerely-held idea, however unscriptural it may be, is acceptable ("to be honored").

B. The content of the task force report demonstrates that its conclusions – i.e., the primacy of institutional unity and its recommendations, and local option regarding "essential standards" – are grounded not in Scripture and the historic creeds and confessions that the task force report says it affirms, but in the various religious experiences of members of the task force. What is being affirmed *is not necessarily the fact that underlies an affirmation, but the person who makes the affirmation.* Thus, in affirming "Jesus is Lord," the task force is not necessarily affirming the fact that Jesus is Lord, but celebrating the fact that some of its members who are loved and respected believe Jesus is Lord.

(1) Further complicating the matter, how one member defines "Lord" may be very different from the way another member defines that title. Jesus himself was clear on that point: "Not everyone who says to me, 'Lord, Lord,' will enter the kingdom of heaven, but the one who does the will of my Father who is in heaven. On that day many will say to me, 'Lord, Lord, did we not prophesy in your name, and cast out demons in your name, and do many mighty works in your name?' And then will I declare to them, 'I never knew you; depart from me, you workers of lawlessness.' Everyone then who hears these words of mine and does them will be like a wise man who built his house on the rock" (Matthew 7:21-24).

(2) The task force abandons the clear word of Scripture when discussing "sexuality and ordination" (line 577 ff). Notice the source material that it cites:

a) "We explored a range of opinions on issues of human sexuality" (line 583). Here, the task force reveals that its source is itself, its own individual and corporate opinions, forgetting Jesus' commendation to Peter: "Blessed are you, Simon Bar-Jonah! For flesh and blood has not revealed this to you, but my Father who is in heaven" (Matthew 16:17). The task force's "opinions" on the matter of human sexuality are mere expressions of flesh and blood, rather than the Word of God.

b) "Though we have shared some of our personal opinions and positions, we focused our studies primarily on the written work of Christian scholars and denominational commissions and assemblies. We read and discussed a diverse collection of theological and biblical writings on these topics. We benefited greatly from this way of grappling with issues and we commend it to the church" (lines 584-587). This is more flesh and blood.

c) Having surveyed the landscape, the task force expresses "surprise" at "how often writers on all sides of the questions bolstered their arguments with appeals to natural law (theological reasoning based on the orders of nature), which is not traditionally a central theme in Protestant theology" (footnote 21, page 16). Had the task force paid closer attention to Scripture, it might have noted that Romans 1 speaks of unnatural acts such as homoerotic behavior precisely in terms of the orders of creation. Historically, this Romans 1 theme has commanded a place of high honor in Protestant theology.

d) The task force finally concludes – contrary to the overwhelming testimony of Biblical scholarship through the ages – that "perspectives on questions of sexuality, ordination and same-gender covenantal relationships are rich and complex, and our fellow task force members who hold these views are sincere, faithful, and guided by Scripture" (lines 686-689). Thus, the task force suggests that "yes/no" answers to these complex matters be replaced with "both/and" answers, a solution that Scripture universally condemns.

3) In its reflections on Scripture, a part of the process in which the task force purportedly developed its conclusions, the members of the task force seriously misread Paul's letter to the Ephesians in drawing only from the first three chapters, which emphasize the unity of the church. This is an inappropriate use of Scripture that

violates historic Reformed principles of interpretation that, ironically, the task force specifies and affirms in another section of its report (lines 533-541).

a) Even in its reference to chapters 1-3, the task force abandons its initial and primary focus on the Triune God, who "chose us in him before the foundation of the world, *that we should be holy and blameless before him*" (Ephesians 1:4, emphasis added). Clearly, in this opening statement, Paul's letter ties right faith to a righteous, moral pattern of living, a connection that the task force unfortunately has ignored. The task force report emphasizes unity, but avoids obedience.

b) After citing unity language – e.g., "For he himself is our peace, who has made us both one and has broken down in his flesh the dividing wall of hostility by abolishing the law of commandments and ordinances. ... So then you are no longer strangers and aliens, but you are fellow citizens with the saints and members of the household of God...," (Ephesians 2:14-19) – the task force abandons reliance on Paul's letter to the Ephesians.

c) The task force thereby misses the great "Therefore" in Chapter Four. The chapter begins by urging Christians "*to walk in a manner worthy of the calling to which you have been called*" (Ephesians 4:1, emphasis added). It then proceeds to spell out the nature of this life to which we have been called: "Now this I say and testify in the Lord, that *you must no longer walk as the Gentiles do*, in the futility of their minds" (Ephesians 4:17, emphasis added), and: "*They have become callous and have given themselves up to sensuality, greedy to practice every kind of impurity*. But that is not the way you learned Christ! – assuming that you have heard about him and were taught in him, as the truth is in Jesus, to put off your old self, which belongs to your former manner of life and is corrupt through deceitful desires, and to be renewed in the spirit of your minds, and to *put on the new self, created after the likeness of God in true righteousness and holiness*" (Ephesians 4:19-24, emphasis added).

d) Finally, Paul brings the focus to the issue of sexual ethics: "But sexual immorality and all impurity or covetousness must not even be named among you, as is proper among saints. ... For you may be sure of this, that everyone who is sexually immoral or impure, or who is covetous (that is, an idolater), has no inheritance in the kingdom of Christ and God" (Ephesians 5:3ff). Note that Paul *relates sexual immorality to idolatry, just as he does in the first chapter of Romans, wherein he specifies homosexual behavior as evidence of idolatry (the creature having assumed the role of the Creator).*

C. The core of the task force's "community-building" experiment is relational, a human process of mutual affirmation in which "loving" others involves affirming the integrity of their "core convictions" – even if one does not agree with those convictions and even if those convictions are contrary to Scripture. Thus, all propositions are regarded as true (in the eyes of those who affirm them) and none is false (as long as someone in the group affirms them as true). This postmodern worldview infects the entire report, *including its theological affirmations,* because it renders language meaningless, thereby throwing into question the very affirmations that the task force makes in the body of its report.

In the theological section of the report, for example, the task force affirms the Nicene Creed. Certainly, Christians who stand with the historic witness of the church applaud this affirmation, but in light of the task force's postmodern assumptions and methodologies, the reader cannot be confident that he or she knows what the task force means when it affirms the Nicene Creed.

a) We recall, for example, that Professor Douglas Ottati – who affirms a Christ-concept, albeit not the Jesus Christ who is revealed in Scripture – says he can affirm the Nicene Creed as long as his is not "an ontological affirmation" (*Jesus Christ and Christian Vision;* Fortress Press; Minneapolis; 1989). But the creed's declaration that Jesus Christ is "of one substance with the Father" becomes meaningless if it has no ontological reference. Clearly, Ottati is affirming *the language* of the creed, but *assigning a different meaning* to it.

b) By elevating abstractions and avoiding absolutes, the task force is able to arrive at a position in which each person in the group could affirm his or her own truth: "We have not compromised our convictions or commitments" (lines 413-414). Similarly, in line 422, the task force says "our respect for differing perspectives has deepened." Herein, the task force demonstrates that its focus is *not on the proposition* (is it true or is it false?), *but on the person* who holds it.

D. Peace, unity and purity are derivative, not primary values. Like happiness, they are not human achievements, but gifts to those who are in right relationship with the Triune God of grace, a relationship that encompasses both faith and "doing the will of the Father."

The task force affirms this in principle: "our shared conviction that the church's peace, unity, and purity are the results not of human efforts but rather of what God has given in Jesus Christ through the gracious work of the Spirit" (lines 474-476); but then proceeds to ignore what it affirms by seeking political solutions (negotiated acquiescence to divergent convictions) to the denomination's theological/ethical dysfunction.

In this regard, we are reminded of Puritan theologian John Owen's statement: "See in the meantime that your faith brings forth obedience and God in due time will cause it to bring forth peace."[1]

E. The task force lifts up the person of Jesus Christ, rightly affirming his full humanity and full divinity, but, in effect, ignores his Lordship and his requirements. This leads the task force to a truncated statement of faith that results in undefined ethical abstractions rather than the ethical particularity that is clearly revealed in the Word of God. Some of those abstractions are as follows:

1) The Lord's Supper "dignifies our diversity, seals our unity, and even reverses our assumptions about our own and others' acceptability" (lines 130-131). What is the meaning of "diversity" that the task force affirms in this statement? Is this national, racial, gender, or socio-political-economic class diversity? Or does this "diversity" include a range of behavior, including behavior that Scripture specifically proscribes? The task force does not tell us, leaving us to "dignify" a diversity that has no specific referent and, therefore, no meaning.

2) The task force includes in its report a section on "discipline," in which it affirms the principle of "leading holy and disciplined lives" (line 220). But nowhere does the task force tell us what discipline means or how it is to be achieved. Notably missing is Scripture affirmed as the benchmark for determining the standard by which human action is assessed. Obedience to Jesus Christ and Biblical ethics is missing. Instead, we are given human values without any Scriptural definition as to what those values mean.

---

1. Owen, John; *The Complete Works of John Owen*; (Banner of Truth Trust; Edinburgh; 1996); Volume VI, "A Practical Exposition Upon Psalm 130."

Examples in the report include "selflessness," "piety," "simplicity," "self discipline," "life of integrity," and the pursuit of "faithful lives that do not "demonstrate licentious behavior" (line 661).

3) A discerning reader will spot the huge loophole in these abstractions, since one could argue that persons who engage in adultery or homoerotic activity, but do so with one rather than multiple partners, are living "faithful lives" that do not "demonstrate licentious behavior." This argument, made publicly by some task force members prior to and during their service on the task force, is precisely what the 1991 General Assembly Task Force on Human Sexuality advocated in its recommendation that the denomination allow for homosexual behavior and some forms of heterosexual adultery. What the task force artfully avoids is the fact that, according to Scripture, *some behaviors are inherently wrong*, whether or not they are "faithfully" enacted.

4) The task force encourages Presbyterians to be engaged in "working for justice" (line 238). Nowhere in the document is justice defined. Is the "justice" that it envisions:

a) commercial (as in giving a person his due);

b) retributive or remedial (as in dealing with acts that offend societal standards);

c) distributive (as in the proper allocation of the world's resources);

d) a synonym for righteousness, as the word often is employed in the Old Testament;

e) a synonym for equality, a view that plays a central – and often unexamined – role in modern liberal thinking; or

f) a code word for defining sexual relations, as in the "justice/love" mantra found in the 1991 Human Sexuality report, wherein sexual activities between consenting adults were regarded as "just" because no coercion was involved?

The task force does not answer these questions. Instead, it leaves us with an abstraction capable of multiple and often mutually exclusive definitions. For example, if a teacher gave identical grades to two students whose academic performance is substantially different, the teacher's commitment to "equality" would, in this instance, be unjust.

In lines 250-256, the task force's concept of justice appears to take shape; namely the notion that justice somehow is associated with equality, the equal distribution of the world's resources.

We see this suggestion in its adulation of two liberationist documents, the Belhar Confession and the Korea declaration. These documents were employed in a call for the redistribution of property and power, justifying if necessary the use of force to achieve it. It was this view of justice that led the Presbyterian Church (USA) to support and fund terrorist Robert Mugabe's guerrilla war in Zimbabwe, and Marxist Daniel Ortega's dictatorship in Nicaragua.

5) The task force makes extensive use of categories – e.g., "liberal," "conservative," "progressive," "evangelical," "moderate," etc. – with no clear definition or examination of these positions *per se*. Rather, the focus is only on "the pain" experienced by persons who are labeled and thereby excluded.

F. The process utilized in generating the report is proffered to the General Assembly as a model for replication among all governing bodies. This process, based on a group's self-consciousness rather than Scripture, is deeply flawed.

1) The task force declares: "This entire report has as its premise that a season of discernment is due in the church, one that all of the task force's recommendations are intended to support" (line 1497). The task force fails to recognize the fact that the Presbyterian Church (USA) has been actively engaged in sexuality discussions since the General Assembly meeting in 1976. For nearly 30 years, the denomination has been engaged in a "season of discernment."

2) The task force recommends that all governing bodies engage in this "season of discernment" and "follow the example of the task force" in its "community building" and "collaborative effort" (line 1086). The purpose of discernment is to make a decision but, after years of using its form of "discernment," the task force has arrived at no consensus and no decision. The task force admits that no member has changed his or her "core convictions." Thus, one must conclude that the method of discernment chosen by this task force has been patently unsuccessful. On what basis should the church replicate this documented failure?

3) The task force affirms that it was directed "to devise 'an instru-

ment and a process' by which means the church can discern and discuss matters that unite and divide it" (lines 1093-1094). Throughout its "process," however, the task force has failed to frame a single issue to be discerned. What are the questions that it calls on the church to discern? Nothing concrete appears in the task force's report or recommendations.

II. Governance and Polity Considerations

The task force report's proposed recommendation #5, set forth in lines 1176-1450, would violate the Constitution of the PC(USA).

Recommendation #5 proposes that the General Assembly adopt an authoritative interpretation of G-6.0108 in the *Book of Order* that would allow a governing body to decide whether an explicit constitutional standard is an "essential of the Reformed faith and polity" to which the presbytery must yield.

A. The task force recommendation would repeal the Authoritative Interpretation already issued by the General Assembly Permanent Judicial Commission that states the relation of G-6.0106b and G-6.0108; namely, that G-6.0106b overrides any ordaining body's discretion in determining standards for the sexual behavior of persons to be ordained.

Although the recommendation says it does not intend to "change" either G-6.0106b or the Authoritative Interpretation of 1978 that preceded G-6.0106b (lines 1347-1350), the report immediately goes on to how that provision of the constitution could be determined by an ordaining body as not being applicable if it so chose (lines 1359-1362).

1) The task force tries to justify this overruling of a constitutional standard by a governing body on the grounds that the relationship between G-6.0108 and "other" sections of the *Book of Order* "has become unclear" (lines 1256-57). The two examples of confusion it gives are that "some" governing bodies say they have the right to overlook "certain" churchwide standards, while "some interpreters" insist that the provisions of the Constitution that govern sexual behavior supersede the right of installing bodies to decide the fitness of candidates for ordination (lines 1257-1262). These opposing viewpoints presented as rationale do exist, but the church has clearly spoken numerous times over the years and said

that the former opinion claiming the right to overlook homosexual behavior is wrong and that the latter understanding is correct. It is not that confusion exists; rather, it is that some people refuse to acquiesce to the authority of the larger church.

2) The most recent declaration is the General Assembly Permanent Judicial Commission ruling in *Londonderry Presbyterian Church v. Presbytery of Northern New England* (decided in July 2000, reported to the 2002 General Assembly). That ruling specifically states that there is no contradiction between G-6.0108 (the section the task force's recommendation wants to "interpret") and G-6.0106b (the standard that supersedes the discretion of governing bodies on matters of sexual behavior). The presbytery in that case argued that, "G-1.0301a and G-6.0108 affirm freedom of conscience with respect to matters addressed by G-6.0106b." The General Assembly Permanent Judicial Commission rejected that assertion, saying that tensions between provisions are to be resolved to give effect to all provisions. The ruling went on to say that G-6.0106b is a qualification established by the whole church, and that the constitution allowed the church to declare the qualifications of its ministers and members. No governing body or judicial commission may declare a properly adopted provision of the Constitution to be invalid, the ruling said, adding: "The only appropriate avenue to change or remove a provision of the *Constitution* is through the process for amendment provided within the *Constitution* itself."

3) The Permanent Judicial Commission then spent some paragraphs in its ruling exploring the paradox of Christian liberty within the covenant church community. It explored our Reformed tradition, which permits a person to hold ideas that contravene a provision of the constitution, but forbids the person from doing an act violating the provision. The decision points to G-6.0108 as echoing those very principles and condemns a declaration by a governing body "not to comply with the *express corporate judgment* of the Church in an explicit *constitutional provision...*" (emphasis added).

4) The Constitution of the Presbyterian Church (USA) provides two ways for an authoritative interpretation to be rendered – by the General Assembly or through a decision of the Permanent Judicial Commission (*Book of Order* G-13.0103r). If the interpretation proposed by the task force were adopted, it would repeal the

Londonderry case, since the "most recent interpretation" of a provision is binding.

[Two famous cases on "essential" ordination standards are those of *Maxwell v. Presbytery of Pittsburgh* (UPCNA Minutes, 1975, p. 254) and *Rankin v. National Capital Union Presbytery* (UPCNA Minutes, 1981, p.113). They are of interest in setting out the constitutional understanding of presbytery discretion and its limits in ordination, but their holdings are not directly applicable to G-6.0108 or G-6.0106b, as both of those sections were adopted after 1983.]

B. The task force recommendation would violate the understanding of the constitutional process for change reached by the Special Commission of 1925 with respect to setting ordination standards.

If the substance of the G-6.0106b prohibition were embodied solely in a case of the General Assembly Permanent Judicial Commission or the Authoritative Interpretation of 1993 without a constitutional section, Recommendation #5 would not violate the Constitution. That, however, is not the case. G-6.0106b is part of the Constitution, and the task force recommendation would violate the Constitution.

1) The task force report mentioned a number of controversies about the understanding of ordination in Presbyterian history. It failed, however, to explore or apply the most recent and *still-controlling* episode.

In the 1920s, a major controversy erupted in the United Presbyterian Church (USA) (the northern branch from the 1861 split until its 1983 reunion with the Presbyterian Church US to form the present Presbyterian Church (USA)). The General Assembly had adopted interpretations of doctrines in 1910, 1916 and 1923, setting out particular understandings such as the virgin birth of Jesus, the inerrancy of Scripture, the substitutionary nature of atonement, and the bodily resurrection of Jesus and declared them to be essential standards. Within six months of the 1923 General Assembly action, 1,274 ministers had signed the Auburn Affirmation protesting that action as unconstitutional. The signers argued that the only process that could legally bind the church on doctrine was one that amended the Constitution, which required the concurrence of the presbyteries.

At the 1925 General Assembly, commissioners overruled the Presbytery of New York's approval of two men for ordination as ministers. On the basis of the 1923 interpretation of essentials, the

General Assembly held that their failure to affirm the virgin birth of Jesus prevented their qualifying for office (*Gantz v. Synod of New York, re Henry P. Van Dusen and Cedric A. Lehman*, minutes, 1925, p. 83). At that same assembly, a Special Commission was appointed to study and report on "the present spiritual condition of our Church and the causes making for unrest ... that the purity, peace, unity, and progress of the Church may be assured."

The commission, chaired by Henry C. Swearingen, made a final report to the 1927 General Assembly. The report focused on this question: "What authority, if any, does the General Assembly possess for declaring any article to be an essential and necessary one in a sense which renders its statement mandatory and applicable to all cases?" (Minutes, 1927, p. 78).

In answering, the commission pointed out certain facts:

a) The Adopting Act of 1729 provided for the decision of essential articles to be made in specific cases, not for the authority to adopt exact language for application rigidly in each case;

b) Before the adoption of the Constitution in 1789, the (General) Synod was co-equal in authority with the Presbytery, so actions before 1789 do not definitely settle current questions; and

c) The matter to which an article is "essential" is to a system of doctrine taught in Scriptures, not to salvation or citizenship in the Kingdom.

The commission then distinguished the powers of the assembly to make general interpretations versus making judicial decisions in a particular case. It said that the "General Assembly has an undoubted right to interpret the Constitution in declaratory deliverances" on what are essential and necessary articles to bear witness to the corporate faith of the Church. Nevertheless, the commission cautioned against such interpretations: "the exercise of the right may lead, as experience has shown, to disturbing results. ... [M]ost of the ministers and members of our Church will agree that the risk of such action is great, and that the General Assembly may well refrain from taking such a course, *especially as it may be misconstrued as a virtual amending of our organic law by another method than that prescribed by the Constitution*" (Minutes, 1927 p. 81; emphasis added).

When a specific case about an individual's doctrinal beliefs comes before the General Assembly in its judicial capacity, however, the commission said the assembly could not rest on the declaratory deliverance of a former assembly. No, "[a] judicial decision is grounded in the Constitution itself and derives its chief additional support from similar decisions arrived at in the same manner and resting upon the same foundation."

Furthermore, the commission said, if the assembly had the authority to broadly declare an article to be essential, commissioners would have to quote the exact language of the article as it appears in the [Westminster] Confession, not using paraphrases or inferences from the confession.

The commission concluded that these clear principles had served the denomination well for the last 200 years and should continue to be followed to serve its peace, purity and unity. Its report was adopted unanimously, and often has been referred to in church discussions and judicial decisions as determinative of the issue that explicit ordination standards can be set only by constitutional amendment. In *Rankin v. National Capital Union Presbytery* (Minutes, 1981, p. 113), the General Assembly Permanent Judicial Commission referred to the report of the Special Commission of 1925 and said, "It is now considered the authoritative statement of these constitutional principles" (Minutes, 1981, p. 114).

2) The understanding expressed by the report was the basis in 1996 for seven of the 15 members of the General Assembly Permanent Judicial Commission declaring that the 1978 Authoritative Interpretation that homosexual behavior barred a person from ordination was unconstitutional. In the case of *Central Presbyterian Church v. Presbytery of Long Island*, Remedial Case 208-4 (Minutes, 1996), the seven judicial commissioners argued that the Permanent Judicial Commission itself had erred in its decision in *Union Presbyterian Church of Blasdell* (Minutes, 1985, p.121) and subsequent cases. The commissioners' minority opinion stated that the Permanent Judicial Commission had been wrong in treating the 1978 statement as though it were a properly enacted amendment to the Constitution. Alluding to G-6.0108a in the *Book of Order*, their opinion said that the 1978 guidance could not be considered an "essential" of the Reformed faith and polity,

but "a detail on which reasonable people within the Reformed tradition may have honest differences of opinion."

3) It is within the clear memory of many people now in the denomination that the near-majority opinion of the *Central Presbyterian Church* case to reverse the *Blasdell* decision upholding the 1978 Definitive Guidance was the impetus to propose a constitutional amendment setting sexual behavior standards for ordination. The *Central Presbyterian Church* case was decided in October 1995; G-6.0106b was proposed to the 1996 General Assembly and sent out by it to the presbyteries. Opponents on both sides of the debate acknowledged that the amendment's effect would be to set a denomination-wide standard that would bind local ordaining bodies.

4) If the Authoritative Interpretation recommended by the task force were adopted, it would be doing the very thing that was the defect attributed to the 1978 Authoritative Interpretation – *trying to effect change in ordination standards by an authoritative interpretation without using the required constitutional process of an amendment sent to the presbyteries.* Moreover, it would be trying to nullify a clear standard already in place in the constitution and voted on three times in the past nine years. The task force report seeks to elevate the Authoritative Interpretation of Recommendation #5 to a change in the text of the constitution by a process that violates the constitution.

C. The task force recommendation would adopt a "presumption of wisdom" in favor of the ordaining body that would be all but impossible to be overcome in any review by higher governing bodies (lines 1199-1206). Thus, in reality, the decision of the ordaining body regarding whether a standard was an "essential" would be final.

1) Lines 1199-1201 in the task force report set out the aspects of the ordaining decision that a higher governing body would be limited to review – whether the examination was conducted "reasonably, responsibly, prayerfully, and deliberately." The actual *correctness* of the determination is trumped by the *manner* of the determination.

2) As stated in *Simmons v. Presbytery of Suwannee* (Minutes 1985, p. 114), "appellants must overcome a substantial weight of authority that grants broad discretion to the presbytery in [ordination] matters." In fact, most of the cases say that "higher judicatories

should substitute their judgment only for the most extraordinary reasons" (*Rankin*, p. 115), and limit inquiry to whether the record contained sufficient evidence to support the presbytery's action. The language in lines 1203-1206 of the task force's report highlighting the "presumption of wisdom" would make such a high hurdle for the evidence to be overcome as to be almost impossible.

D. The task force recommendation would allow the standards of sexual behavior based on at least 2,000 years of Biblical understanding to be violated by ordaining bodies pending an indeterminate process of discernment (lines 1353-1356).

1) The standard of fidelity in marriage and chastity in singleness that G-6.0106b in the *Book of Order* prescribes is derived from the Scriptures and has been upheld by the Church Universal as true since the birth of the Church at Pentecost. *The Book of Confessions* of the Presbyterian Church (USA) explicitly proffers that standard in at least four of its documents.

2) It is shocking that the task force could propose tolerating the abrogation of those standards "while the debate continues," which it recognizes may be "many years." The damage that would be done to the name of Jesus Christ and to individuals by condoning such sexual license in the "meantime" while the "discernment" continues is incalculable.

E. The task force recommends that the General Assembly "direct" and "urge" governing bodies to "explore the use of alternative forms of discernment and decision-making ..." (line 1150). This recommendation is tantamount to a de facto amendment to the *Book of Order*.

1) In the body of its report, the task force finds favor with non-parliamentary methodologies that "seek constructive, Christ-like alternatives to the 'yes/no' forms in which questions about sexuality, ordination, and same-gender covenantal relations have been put to the church in recent decades" (line 689).

2) The task force declares that "in strategies that offer win-lose options only ... we alienate ourselves from one another," and suggests that, in requiring that clear-cut choices be made, "we deny the gift of the grace of God" (lines 191-194).

3) In *Time for Truth*,[1] theologian Os Guinness speaks directly to

---

1. Guinness, Os; *Time for Truth: Living Free in a World of Lies, Hype & Spin*; (Hourglass Books; Grand Rapids, Mich.; 2000); p. 110.

the task force's aversion to "yes/no" decisions. Guinness says that the ultimate undeniability of truth always confronts us with two choices: "Either we conform the truth to our desires or we conform our desires to the truth." Continuing his commentary, Guinness said, "Kiekegaard was so committed to the responsibility of this choice that he was nicknamed 'Either/Or.' 'I who am called Either/Or,' he once said, 'cannot be at the service of anybody with both/and.'"

4) The Constitution of the Presbyterian Church (USA) makes the following requirement: "Meetings of governing bodies, commissions, and committees shall be conducted in accordance with the most recent edition of *Robert's Rules of Order*, except in those cases where this Constitution provides otherwise" (G.9.0302).

(a) In mandating parliamentary procedure (note the word "shall"), the Constitution recognizes that civilized debate according to established rules of engagement is a tried-and-true method for giving all positions a fair hearing, testing arguments, discerning the truth, and achieving a binding decision.

b) The task force's nurturing of friendships is commendable on a personal level. It may be an excellent model for personal relations if it can be followed in small group settings without forcing participants to conform to a consensus that denies what the Bible clearly affirms.

c) History, however, provides no evidence that small-group consensus methodologies have been successful in large-group settings. Beyond the level of intimate association, interpersonal relationship methodologies breed chaos, and the body politic is rendered unable to make just and binding decisions. This state-of-nature reality has led many civilized cultures to incorporate some form of parliamentary procedure into the discernment and decision-making process.

III. Conclusion

The task force report and its recommendations should be rejected *in toto*. The process utilized in generating this report (and offered to the General Assembly as a model for replication among all governing bodies) and the report itself is made of whole cloth. Were the General Assembly to adopt or approve this report, it would align the Presbyterian Church (USA) not only with a particular document, but with the process that produced it. In offering itself as a model, the task force has declared that its process and product are inseparable.

The task force's methodology and the ideological assumptions that underlie it substitute the self for Scripture. Admittedly, those who read the report from the perspective of a Biblical worldview can find acceptable statements scattered therein. But lifting isolated phrases piecemeal from this whole-cloth document would produce a tattered and incoherent product, certainly nothing from which the denomination can discern the mind of Christ.

The task force report invites replacement, not repair. That replacement must begin at the beginning, with the revealed Word of God. Aside from that Word, we cannot have substance, because "all things were made through him, and without him was not any thing made that was made" (John 1:1). To anchor the report in the experience of self – albeit a corporate self comprised of friendly and well-meaning people – constitutes an exercise that is unworthy of Christ's Church.

The task force's replacement must follow Scripture from beginning to end, from a Biblical theology to the ethic that flows logically, necessarily and consistently out of that theology. Admittedly, this congruity will cause discomfort, "pain," and a sense of exclusion for those who will not live according to God's Word. Exposed to the language of a therapeutic culture, we can understand the task force's decision to avoid this pain. Scripture and our own experience, however, teach us that pain can be providential. It can move us to repentance that leads to restoration and righteous living.

Loving others does not require affirming their opinions or convictions if such are unscriptural, unethical, or harmful to themselves or society. Loving others by listening to their convictions is an appropriate model for human relationships, but governance and leadership require discernment and judgment as to what is true or false, right or wrong.

Replacing a report that was years in the making might be regarded by some as an impossible task. Certainly, if one were to repeat the task force's error by beginning again to forge another consensus among radically diverse ideologies and lifestyles, success would be (and should be) impossible.

But with God, all things are possible. The key to this more hopeful future is the phrase "with God." He can do for the Presbyterian Church (USA) what no task force can do. He does not begin where we are, but where he is; and, by the grace of our Lord Jesus Christ in the power of his Holy Spirit, that is exactly where he invites us to be.

In *The Pursuit of God,* A.W. Tozer[1] describes how the many diverse instruments of an orchestra achieve unity. They do not discover the right tone by conferring with one another. Instead, the pitch of each instrument is adjusted in relation to one true tone, a tuning fork. It is in congruence with that single standard that they find their way to one another. Therein lies a parable for those who would seek the peace, unity and purity of the Church.

"The grass withers, the flower fades, but the word of our God will stand forever."[2]

---

1. Tozer, A.W.; *The Pursuit of God: The Human Thirst for the Divine*; (Christian Publications; Harrisburg, Pa.; 1994).

2. Isaiah 40:8.

Appendix Four

A Common Statement on the Report of the Theological Task Force On the Peace, Unity and Purity of the Presbyterian Church (USA)

A Common Statement on the Report of the Theological Task Force On the Peace, Unity and Purity of the Presbyterian Church (USA)

The General Assembly Theological Task Force on Peace, Unity, and Purity of the Church has issued a report to the denomination, requesting that Presbyterians reflect upon its findings in a period of discernment. We, representatives of renewal organizations in the Presbyterian Church (USA), accept the Task Force invitation and have gathered in Chicago for the purpose of studying and responding to the Task Force report.

Task Force members worked long and hard and are to be thanked for their efforts to create an instrument whose purpose is to help the church discern how to live in peace, unity, and purity. With them, we are grieved by our denomination's decline and disunity. We had hoped and prayed that from the Task Force report we would hear a witness to the Word of the Lord that would speak to the needs of our church.

In parts of this report, we do hear a witness to the Word of God. Certain statements affirm God's eternal Triune identity, the singular saving Lordship of Jesus Christ, the authority of Holy Scripture, and the necessity of living a disciplined and holy life.

In spite of these valuable affirmations, we conclude with regret that the report has not given the church a consistently clear witness to the Word of God. Taken as a whole, it constitutes a blend of truth and error that, if adopted, will undermine the church's purity and exacerbate the denomination's disunity. Indeed, it will promote schism by permitting the disregard of clear standards of Scripture and the Constitution of the

Presbyterian Church (USA).

This report will not promote the peace and unity of the church.

The report promotes radical change while claiming to make no change. Recommendation 5 will bring about denominational fragmentation through *de facto* local option. Ordaining bodies would be authorized to disregard explicit constitutional standards, including but not limited to the fidelity/chastity requirement in G-6.0106b.

The proposed authoritative interpretation would reverse the will of the church without consulting the church through constitutional amendment. Thus, it does not respect the Presbyterian way of delineating and maintaining boundaries for our community. Although higher governing bodies would be permitted to review the work of ordaining bodies, they would not be under any obligation to ensure compliance with confessional standards specifically singled out by amendment and constitutionally required of all governing bodies. Indeed, they would be encouraged to "honor" that work with a "presumption of wisdom." The proposed authoritative interpretation, which was intended to advance church unity, will further divide the church by inviting all ordaining bodies to do "what is right in their own eyes" (Judges 21:25). They will have the right to convert a mandated "shall" in the *Book of Order* to a merely permissible "may" or "might," even though the *Book of Order* carefully distinguishes between these ways of speaking.

In addition, the Task Force report will not promote unity in the worldwide church. Our brothers and sisters in the non-Western church – the majority church – find our moral confusion troubling. Our relationship with them has been harmed and would be further harmed by the adoption of this report.

The report will not promote the purity of the church.

For the past quarter-century, the Presbyterian Church (USA) has repeatedly expressed its conviction regarding God's will in matters of sexual morality. The report subverts these core sexual standards of behavior that are grounded in Scripture by substituting sincerely expressed personal opinions for rigorous Biblical exegesis that has been confirmed by centuries of church tradition.

The report accepts conflicting interpretations of Scripture without doing the hard work of helping the church to assess the respective merits of these interpretations. The report proposes compromising the one Word of God with "words," by replacing the witness of Scripture with the product of dialogue. By replacing the authority of Scripture with a consensus-building process, the report separates the church from its only real source of purity, Jesus Christ. The Lord of the church prays for our purity, "Sanctify them by the truth; your word is truth" (John 17:17).

These observations lead us to conclude that the Task Force report does not provide what the church needs at this critical juncture in our life together. The report will not promote the peace, unity, and purity for which the Savior prays, for which we hope, and to which we are committed.

Because we cannot commend the whole report to the church, our renewal organizations will offer resources to assist the church in discerning a better way to seek its peace, unity, and purity.

May the grace of our Lord Jesus Christ, the love of God, and the fellowship of the Holy Spirit be with us all.

Signed by:

Rev. Dr. Jerry Andrews, co-moderator, Presbyterian Coalition

Ms. Gabrielle S. Avedian, Presbyterian Forum

Rev. Anita Bell, co-moderator, Presbyterian Coalition

Rev. Dr. Jim Berkley, interim director, Presbyterian Action for Faith and Freedom

Elder Marie Bowen, executive director, Presbyterians Pro-Life

Rev. Katie Brandt, executive director, Presbyterian Forum

Rev. Dr. Richard Burnett, Erskine Seminary

Rev. Sue Cyre, executive director, Presbyterians for Faith, Family and Ministry

Rev. Dr. Gerrit Dawson, pastor, First Presbyterian Church, Baton Rouge, Louisiana

Rev. Tom Edwards, executive director, New Wineskins Initiative

Rev. Don Elliot, president, Presbyterians Pro-Life

Rev. Dennis Finnegan, vice president, Presbyterian Reformed Ministries International

Dr. Robert Gagnon, Pittsburgh Theological Seminary

Elder Peggy Hedden, chair, Presbyterian Lay Committee

Elder Bob Howard, Presbyterian Lay Committee

Rev. Dr. Brad Long, executive director, Presbyterian Reformed

Ministries International

Rev. Dr. Peyton Johnson, pastor, Lakeside Presbyterian Church,
Tarpon Springs, Florida

Rev. Dr. Mark Patterson, pastor, Community Presbyterian Church,
Ventura, California

Rev. Cindy Strickler, Presbyterian Reformed Ministries International

Rev. James Tony, Presbyterian Coalition

Rev. Parker Williamson, executive director, Presbyterian Lay Committee

Elder Alan Wisdom, interim president, Institute on Religion
and Democracy

October 10, 2005
Chicago, Illinois

Bibliography

The Holy Bible, English Standard Version™ (Wheaton, Illinois; Crossway Bibles, a division of Good News Publishers; 2001).

Bailey, Kenneth E.; "The Structure of I Corinthians and Paul's Theological Method with Special Reference to 4:17;" *Novum Testamentum*; XXV 2 (1983); pp. 152-181.

"Paul's Theological Foundation for Human Sexuality: I Cor. 6:9-20 in the Light of Rhetorical Criticism;" *Theological Review* (Near East School of Theology); (April 1980); pp. 27-41.

"Recovering the Poetic Structure of I Corinthians i 17 v 2: A Study in Text and Commentary;" *Novum Testamentum* 17; (October 1975); pp. 265-296.

Barth, Karl; *Church Dogmatics*; (T&T Clark Publishers; Edinburgh; 1969).

Conflict in the Church; (*Leben und Glauben*; July 10, 1937).

Calvin, John; *Institutes of the Christian Religion*; Beveridge, Henry (translator) (Grand Rapids, Mich.; William B. Eerdmans Publishing Company; 1990).

Edwards, James R.; *Is Jesus the Only Savior?* (Grand Rapids, Mich.; William B. Eerdmans Publishing Company; 2005).

Ffinch, Michael; *G.K. Chesterton: A Biography* (San Francisco; Harper & Row; 1986).

Gagnon, Robert; *The Bible and Homosexual Practice* (Nashville, Tenn.; Abingdon Press; 2001).

Guinness, Os; *Time for Truth: Living Free in a World of Lies, Hype & Spin*; (Hourglass Books; Grand Rapids, Mich.; 2000).

Kittel, Gerhard and Friedrich, Gerhard (editors), and Bromiley, Geoffrey W. (translator); *The Theological Dictionary of the New Testament* (Grand Rapids, Mich.; William B. Eerdmans Publishing Company; 1977).

Newbigin, Lesslie; *The Light Has Come* (Grand Rapids, Mich.; William B. Eerdman's Publishing Company; 1984).

Ottati, Douglas F.; "Some Characteristics of Progressive Presbyterian Theologies;" Web site of the Witherspoon Society.

Owen, John; *The Complete Works of John Owen*; (Banner of Truth Trust; Edinburgh; 1996); Volume VI, "A Practical Exposition Upon Psalm 130."

Smith, Christian and Lundquist, Melinda; *Soul Searching: The Religious and Spiritual Lives of American Teenagers*; (Oxford University Press; New York; 2005).

Tozer, A.W.; *The Pursuit of God: The Human Thirst for the Divine;* (Christian Publications; Harrisburg, Pa.; 1994).

Turner, Phillip; "An Unworkable Theology," *First Things;* (June/July 2005); pp. 10-12.

ABOUT THE AUTHORS

The Rev. Dr. Gerrit Scott Dawson is senior pastor of First Presbyterian Church in Baton Rouge, Louisiana, and previously served churches in Delaware and North Carolina.

He received a Bachelor of Arts degree with honors in English from Vanderbilt University, a Master of Divinity degree from Princeton Theological Seminary and a Doctor of Ministry degree from Reformed Theological Seminary in Charlotte, N.C.

Actively involved in seminar and retreat leadership, Dawson also has cultivated a writing ministry that includes, with Steve Strickler, *Living Stories*, an elementary Sunday school curriculum based on 125 core Bible stories; numerous articles for *Weavings: A Journal of the Christian Spiritual Life*; and a contribution to the spiritual formation program *Companions in Christ*.

He also is the author or editor of the books *Jesus Ascended: The Meaning of Christ's Continuing Incarnation; I Am With You Always: Meeting Jesus in Every Season of Life; A Passion for Christ: The Vision that Ignites Ministry – Thomas Torrance, James B. Torrance, and David W. Torrance (with Jock Stein); Love Bade Me Welcome: Daily Readings with George Herbert; Called by a New Name: Becoming What God Has Promised; Writing on the Heart: Inviting Scripture to Shape Daily Life;* and *Heartfelt: Finding Our Way Back to God.*

He and his wife, Rhonda, have four children: Micah, Leah, Jacob and Mary-Emeline.

The Rev. Dr. Mark R. Patterson is senior pastor of Community Presbyterian Church in Ventura, California.

He received a Bachelor of Arts degree from Whitworth College, a Master of Divinity degree from Princeton Theological Seminary and a Doctor of Philosophy degree (systematic theology/history of doctrine) from King's College, London.

Actively involved in Bible and theology teaching, conference and retreat leadership, Patterson also has cultivated a writing ministry that includes articles in numerous publications.

He also is an adjunct professor theology at Fuller Theological Seminary.

He and his wife, Linda Lee, have two daughters, Sarai and Kalie

Printed in the United States
43753LVS00003B/1-159